TRIPPIN' ON THE SOFA DURING THE DAMNDEMIC

Praise for TRIPPIN' ON THE SOFA DURING THE DAMNDEMIC

"Dr. Atkinson-Alston's book presents all-too-common occurrences in the workplace. These dilemmas are the type that can derail a career or cause sleepless nights and stress-related problems at home as well. This book can help readers find tools to cope with similar real-life situations using self-reflective and mindful thinking."

Joan Thomas-Spiegel, PhD
Retired Researcher and Psychology Professor

"I recommend this book to scholars, educators, health care professionals, historians, and politicians. After reading this book, you will gain knowledge from a different perspective, it will strengthen your beliefs on this topic, learn a new point of view about the sad experience this pandemic has on people of color."

Marlon R. Hall, EdD
Retired Community College President

"Thought provoking, reflective, and an impactful easy must-read for millennials and Gen Xers to be called to action. Anyone who has been hit hard by this pandemic; whether it be financially, emotionally, or socially, can benefit from this book. It gives a sense of security that we are not alone in our struggles and provides motivation to keep striving forward in these trying times."

Joseph Barakat, BA-Communications
Youth Soccer Coach-Shaping the Future

"Wow! After starting this book, I could not put it down. This book is very reader-friendly and timely. It is a hidden gem about how we can positively uplift and support each other during this pandemic that has upended our lives. Anyone working with others (virtually or from home) should read it. By the end of the book, you will thank Dr. Atkinson-Alston for sharing typical workplace dilemmas that are real career challenges and for taking the time to write the extremely helpful end of chapter reflections."

Yasmin Delahoussaye, EdD
Retired College President

TRIPPIN' ON THE SOFA DURING THE DAMNDEMIC

Dr. Stephanie A. Atkinson-Alston
#1 International Best Selling Author

DEDICATION

This book is dedicated to Keith Michael Joseph, Jr. (02/08/1989-04/19/2020), and the many others who lost their lives to Covid-19. And to those who lost their lives or livelihood to social injustices in 2020.

Amaya, you are the reason that I do what I do.

Grateful, Dr. A

Acknowledgements

To always show up, unapologetic, and authentically me as I strive toward perfecting the call to my vocation.

Thank you for the gentle reminders along the way:

TJ for reminding me of my power and purpose in creative story- telling to help others. For our many adventures in life, including driving on the opposite side of the road in foreign countries. Always rest in your own peace.

Dr. G. for assuring me that doing the right thing is the only thing.

Brothers Barakat and Benjamin, Sisters Dorothy, Shirley, Vanessa, and Wanda for reminding me who is my true source, strength, and salvation.

DP, a coach's coach, thank for everything and always keeping it real. And to the awesome and amazing team for making my dreams become reality.

About the Author

#1 International Best-Selling Author of What They Won't Teach You In Grad School, Dr. Stephanie A. Atkinson-Alston is an entrepreneur, professional development, and leadership evidence-based coach. As the Director of An Atkinson Alston Production, she engages clients through coaching to move them to their desired goals.

"Moving forward each day may mean that the step you take today maybe half of the steps that you took yesterday. Nevertheless, it is a step forward."

Dr. Stephanie A. Atkinson-Alston

Contents

Introduction

When 2020 started, it held the promise that every new year contains. I had goals and aspirations of attacking 2020 with the normal vigor I use every January 1. There is something about New Year's Day that you recognize as a time for a new start. You have the holidays to catch your breath from getting through the past year. Having evaluated your accomplishments from the preceding twelve months, you launch into the new year with bucketloads of optimism. That's how I approach a new year, and I believe many people consider it the same way. Plus, 2020 was even the start of a new decade where you begin to think about what you want to accomplish over the next ten years!

Then COVID-19 took over the world. Mundane things we took for granted, like browsing around a store or going on vacation, stopped happening. What mask to wear before you left your home became the new fashion question. The way we approached work became something that most people didn't recognize anymore. Those who yearned for more time to bond with their family got so much more than they ever thought possible. For some, it became the old saying of "Be careful what you ask for!"

On top of the pandemic offered by COVID-19, the United States was in a volatile state where equality of race and gender were causing explosive discussions and demonstrations. Politics were a mess, and it seemed like people chose sides on any argument with such a passion that they wouldn't even listen to an opposing point of view. Add to that losing national treasures like Congressman John Robert Lewis and Supreme Court Justice Ruth Bader

Ginsburg, and the world appeared to be spiraling off its axis, making you wonder when the next disaster occurred.

In the middle of this craziness, I tried to think of a way to bring some meaning and order to what we were all experiencing. I would find myself having internal discussions, trying to make sense of one of the worse years in the past century. I had the brainstorm of writing about those debates going on in my head. I decided to bring back Felicia and Trey, the central characters of my previous book, What They Won't Teach You in Grad School. I believed their interaction as they dealt with the pandemic and the other events of 2020 would strike a chord with readers and help others sort through their emotions of the year's events.

Often when we are in the midst of difficult circumstances, we don't have time to reflect. We are reacting the best we can to make it through whatever storm we find ourselves in. The pandemic has been brutal. For one thing, at a time when everybody wants something yesterday, and the big new item is always on the horizon, the pandemic taught us patience. Rarely have so many people in the 20th and 21st century had to wait for something to run its course. Furthermore, COVID has been like a marathon where the finish line keeps moving. At the time of this writing, vaccines were being developed, and the country returning back to "normal" wasn't in the near future or if ever.

There are lessons to be learned from 2020, and that's one purpose of the book. We need to reflect on how we had to change our entire lifestyles to maintain a degree of function and sanity. Some of our careers will be indelibly changed by COVID, or at the very least, how we do our work. I want readers to reflect on Felicia and Trey's discussions and think about where you were when dealing with some of the same issues.

Finally, I want you to all give yourself a pat on the back for getting through the past year. We still have a way to go, but the human spirit couldn't be doused because of a virus, political turmoil, issues surrounding race and gender, and unfortunately, losing people to this awful curse of nature. I would love to hear if you see yourself in any of the situations, I talk about in Trippin' on the Sofa During the Damndemic. Stay safe and stay strong!

Chapter 1
Covid Creates a New Normal
#Damndemic

I t was early April 2020, and Felicia sat down with a thud on her chair in her home office. She should be at her department conference room at the university by now, drinking tea and starting a staff meeting to continue planning the next five years of development at the college. She was now the CFO of the university, and she took her job seriously. She relished working with faculty and staff members across the campus as she guided the school's fiscal success. Her last two years went well, and she wanted to be in her office, dressed in her favorite Armani suit as she prepared to keep her financial plan firing on all cylinders.

Instead, Felicia looked down at the bunny slippers a nephew gave her for Christmas. They poked out from her pajama bottoms, which didn't match the New York Mets sweatshirt she wore. The campus had closed down two weeks ago as COVID-19 stretched across the land and created havoc from airline travel to buying groceries.

Felicia laughed at herself because she realized it only took a couple of weeks working from home for her habits to change completely. Normally, she would have been up at 5:00, at the gym by 6:00, shower, and change there before whisking off to her office. With the campus and the gym closed, she wandered into her home office by 8:00 to start working. She could access her files from here and had done a decent job of plowing forward with work. However, some of her staff and other university officials had occasional technical issues, and they were not functioning like a well-oiled machine yet. She had a Zoom meeting scheduled for the end of the preceding day and had to end up punting on it because so many people had trouble connecting.

Looking at her email, she smiled when she saw that Trey had sent her a note. They had met several years ago at a conference and started talking when Trey explained he received his doctorate from the university where Felicia worked. They became friends, and Felicia had visited him and his wife when she was in Chicago last year.

The email said, "Help! I can deal with grad students, but this homeschooling of an eight and a ten-year-old is too much. I need a sanity break. Are you using Zoom? If so, let's schedule a meeting. I'll have my wife watch the kids for an hour. She owes me! Let me know when."

Laughing out loud, Felicia sent a reply to Trey.

At 5:28 in the afternoon, Felicia sat back down in front of her computer screen. She wore leggings from the waist down, but she wore a lovely light blue blouse as a top. This was her third Zoom teleconference of the day. After her first week working from home, it occurred to her that everyone only saw her from the waist up, so there was no need to completely dress for the day.

She clicked on her Zoom meeting and then heard a sound announcing someone else coming online. Since this was only for her and Trey, she was not surprised to see his image flash on the screen. She saw his big smile and noticed he had gotten rid of the dreadlocks he had when she last saw him, and now he had his dark hair cropped close to his head. At the first lunch of the business conference where they met, they realized they were the only two people of color.

Felicia said, "Hey, stranger! How did you manage to get some time for yourself?"

"I had to cover two days of homeschooling for Trevor and Kim while Alyse had a two-day online conference. Originally, it was in Orlando, and we were going to take the kids out of school for a few days. I was going to play with them in Disney World while my wife worked, then do a few days in the parks with all of us. As with just about everything else, that got shot to hell with this pandemic. She has them in the kitchen, helping her with dinner. They all said, 'Hi.'"

"Right back at them," said Felicia. "I've been trying to run my department from home. It has been a slow go, but we seem to be getting better at it each day. I hope it's only temporary."

"I'm thinking we'll be back at our workplaces in about a month," said Trey. "I've only been in my new job for nine months, and now I'm trying to do it from here. Not easy with kids."

"I can only imagine," said Felicia. "How does a professor of economics go to work for an international banking company?" she asked.

"They pay a lot more than a university. Besides, I figure the practical experience will serve me well whenever I start teaching again. Maybe next year, I will see about doing a class somewhere. There are several colleges within driving distance of me. I miss the teaching, so doing a night course would be enjoyable. How's things at the big boy university you are at?"

"It has its challenges, but I am enjoying it. Abruptly shutting down the campus and scrambling to make things work from my staff's homes has been hectic. I believe next week might almost be normal."

"You always were the optimist," said Trey. "I remember that from the first time we met. I still have trouble wrapping my head around a sweet, little Mexican girl going from a soul food restaurant to one of the top colleges in the land."

"First of all, I was never all that sweet. And while I always thought of myself as Mexican American, today I am referred to as Latin X. It's not like they changed the designation of an Irish American or an Italian American to a European American. It was like the powers-that-be were taking my heritage and throwing it in one pot."

"Had did that soul food thing come about? Truthfully, I think of soul food, I think of my people," said Trey.

Felicia chuckled. "If you grew up in Houston, we might have been from the same neighborhood. I loved growing up in a black and brown neighborhood. It was mostly blue-collar workers." She gave a bright smile. "During the year, there would be several Saturday block parties. All the neighbors brought their favorite dishes to share with each other. My African American neighbors would bring fresh fried fish from their recent fishing trips, collard greens, cornbread, green salad, and peach cobbler. Then, us Mexicans would bring beans, rice, carne asada, homemade tortillas, and flan.

"One neighbor had a built-in outdoor oven and grill, where everyone would barbeque various meats like chicken, pork ribs, and carnitas. It was so much fun playing yard games with my friends as the aroma from the grill would make everybody's belly growl. It was great sitting down and sharing so much different food with such diverse neighbors. I was pretty young when I owned the soul food restaurant. In truth, the menu was almost as diverse as the block parties."

Trey said, "Now my stomach is growling thinking about it. Why did you get out?"

"I loved owning my own business, but I wanted to do more. I didn't see myself being the queen of a soul food empire in the future, so I went to college. I had an offer I couldn't refuse and sold my business. I liked school so much that I decided that is the career path I wanted. It's worked out," Felicia said with a smile.

"I'll say," agreed Trey. "I have to tell you, though, that we wouldn't have been in the same neighborhood. I grew up in what we called the "Projects" on the southside of Chicago. Now the term is 'affordable housing.' Back then, the people living there couldn't afford much at all, and the conditions reflected it. My mom was by herself, and it was me, my two brothers, and my sister growing up there. We had to chase the rats away to play on the playground."

"Wow, that had to be awful," said Felicia.

"It was definitely a challenge," said Trey. "Statistically, an African American male from that neighborhood had a great chance to be dead or incarcerated by twenty-five. My family and siblings rallied around me to keep me on the straight and narrow. My oldest brother gave me the 'talk' about how to act if a policeman approached me. I was one of the lucky ones. Between family, teachers, and coaches, I graduated near the top of my class and was a fair football player. That got me to a scholarship. I knew I wasn't big enough or good enough to make the NFL, so I had fun playing football, but concentrated on my studies."

Felicia said, "A real rags to riches story."

"Not so sure about the riches, but I met a great woman, love my kids, and enjoying my job so far. I thought I would stop with my MBA, but the doctorate opportunity came up. Our place is nice where we live, but as the

4

crow flies, it is only eight miles away from the Projects."

"How are you handling the pandemic?" asked Felicia.

"I'm not used to being inside all day. The kids are bouncing off the wall, and Alyse and I spend the evening seeing what we can watch on Netflix. I should be taking the kids out to start playing softball and baseball. This is not how life should be."

"I totally agree," said Felicia, "and I promised myself I was going to take up golf this spring, but that isn't happening for a while. My girlfriend talked me into it."

"I am beginning to call this thing the Damndemic!" exclaimed Trey. It seems like what passed for normal two weeks ago has been gone for a year. If I think too far in the future, I can't even imagine how we can ride this out for months or years."

Felicia visibly shuddered. "Don't even go there. As it was, I was incredibly happy to see your email. As much work as I have, there is a certain loneliness here right now. I am used to being around people all day. I don't even have a cat to keep me company here."

"I know you can handle it," said Trey. "You'll probably thrive in it."

"How can you be sure of that?" asked Felicia.

"Because you have a track record of success. I remember how you told me about navigating the university's hierarchy to get to where you are today. That means you can do it again."

Felicia rubbed her eyes. "Maybe it's because I haven't been sleeping well with all this change, but I don't get what you mean."

Trey took a deep breath and thought for a moment. Felicia could see his face on the screen stare far off for a few seconds. Then, with a shake of his head, Trey returned from wherever he had his mind. "You remember that conference where we met and how we met?"

"Yes, we were the only people of color in the room and started talking to each other."

"Right, and the people at that conference were all pretty great. I don't know about you, but I didn't feel any bias or race issues there."

It was Felica's turn to think for a minute. "No, you're right."

Trey said, "Is it safe to assume that you have felt racial tensions in some places that you went or worked?"

"Of course, I did," she said without even thinking. "A little too much at times."

"I ran into it a lot where I grew up and in school," said Trey. "Sometime around my third year in college, I realized that I had developed a little internal system to deal with adversity. It started because of race issues, but soon I applied when things got tough in football, or I was having difficulty with a class, or my girlfriend blew me off."

"I can't imagine a girl ever blowing you off," said Felicia with a flutter to her eyes and a sardonic smile.

"My buddies used to call me 'Strikeout Trey' in college, and I didn't play baseball. That's why when Alyse came along, I couldn't believe she would stay with me for so long, and even get married. As I think on it, my methodology probably served me well in finding her and keeping her."

Felicia asked, "So what did you do? And is it applicable to the "Damndemic" as you call it?"

"I think it is good for any struggle a person is having. I call it the 4Rs. The first thing you do is spend some time reflecting on past situations. It might not be anything like you are dealing with now. If it is, then that is great, but we all have situations in our life where the degree of stress is the same, even if the circumstances are different. Think about something where you felt the same level of stress or anxiety and remember what you did in that situation. You can extrapolate lessons from those times that you can adapt to what you are currently dealing with now. That begins your process of developing a solution."

"You mean figure out how to deal with this isolation and running a major department based on past successes?" asked Felicia.

"Yes! It could also be a past failure that you learned from when it occurred." Trey took a breath and said, "The next 'R' is reclaiming trust in yourself. It is human nature for our confidence to slip when we do not immediately develop a solution to a problem. We have to remind ourselves we probably solved worse issues, and we can do it again."

"You're making sense," said Felicia. "What's the next 'R'?"

"Rediscovering your self-respect. You can see there is a flow to the method.

Once we trust our talents and abilities again, we have respect for what we can do. When we have self-respect, then retaining a positive attitude and moving forward can transpire. That is the fourth R. That goes a long way to overcoming any obstacle, and I have learned to spread that positiveness around. I send out encouraging texts and messages to friends. One thing about this Damndemic, many of us are in the same boat. It's kind of why I wrote to you."

"Well, sir, I am glad you did. This little chat was certainly a good pick-me-up. I forget that you are a good influence on me. I've learned some helpful things from you."

Trey grinned. "Hey, you've taught me a few things too. Why don't we make this a weekly thing on Zoom? It might very well serve as a mental health check for us."

Felicia clapped her hands. "You are on, Trey. Heck, you gave me something to think about today. Plus, it will help keep me from talking to the walls."

"It is only a problem if they start to talk back," said Trey. "Let's throw a schedule together, so we stick to it."

"Agreed," said Felicia. "Thanks for emailing me this morning, Trey. This has been good."

Courageous Reflections

Now that you have read "COVID Creates a New Normal":

- What resonated with you?

- What caused you to think and ponder?

- What made you curious to investigate further?

- What notes could you jot down?

- The future has always been unknown and unpredictable. What has the Damndemic made you more aware of in your day-to-day life?

- We/you are only in control of our actions and our reactions. How are you responding?

- What action(s)/goal(s) could you take to experience the best outcome(s)?

- What is your plan, and when do you start, and how will you know when you have achieved your goals?

Reflection Notes

_____

_____

_____

_____

_____

_____

_____

_____

_____

_____

_____

_____

_____

_____

_____

_____

_____

_____

_____

Chapter 2
Mindfulness on Steroids
#mindfullness

The alarm on her phone was continuously buzzing. Felicia heard it as she stepped out of the shower. Looking at the alert on her phone, she was surprised to see what time it was already. Walking quickly back to her home office, she went to push the link to enter the Zoom conference. She first put on the camera, and her finger was about to push the "enter" key when she saw herself in the video display. With a shriek, she got out of her chair and moved to the side of the desk. Carefully leaning over, she hit "enter." After a few seconds, she heard Trey's voice.

"Hey, how's it going? Wait a minute – where are you? All I see is a chair."

Felicia said, "Let's just say you almost saw more of me than you bargained for. Keep yourself amused for a few minutes. I didn't want to be late, but my schedule got all out of whack today, thanks to the Damndemic. I was drying off when I saw it was time for our call. I'll be right back."

She dashed to her bedroom, finished drying off, and threw on leggings and a Disney World sweatshirt. She went back and sat behind her desk. She saw her friend was looking a little forlorn. "I'm back," she said.

Trey said, "That's about the fastest I have known a woman to get dressed."

"Hey, don't get all typical man on me," said Felicia with a smile. "It's not like we're going to dinner or something. Besides, this is kinda how I dressed all today. It is the first day in ages that I haven't video chatted with someone. I did have a conference phone call earlier, but I won't even tell you what I wore to that."

"One of the vice presidents here at the bank sent out an email telling us that we should dress as if we are coming to the office. She said that it would put us in a professional frame of mind to do our work, plus we'll be ready whenever we get a last-minute video call Trey commented."

"The university said that to us, too," explained Felicia. "I tried it for three days and thought it was a stupid way to add to my laundry pile. After that, I made sure I at least had a professional shirt or blouse on. Now that I am in my third month of working from home, I keep one next to the desk. I've become quite a quick-change artist."

"That's funny," said Trey, "because that is what I do. Except I get to go into the office two to three times a week. In fact, I only got home a little while ago. Alyse took the kids to visit her sister in the next town, so I was surprised to come home to a quiet house. It's quite the novelty!"

"So, you were at the bank today. What's going on with you? You don't look like a happy camper. You look like you lost your best friend."

"Is it that obvious?" asked Trey.

"Yup! Spill – what's going on?" pressed Felicia.

Trey sat there for a moment, looking at the camera. Felicia could see the stress and unhappiness in his face. Finally, he gave a half-hearted smile and said, "I might as well tell you. That way, I'll get it out of my system before everyone gets back home. Why ruin their night!"

Felicia said, "That's what friends are for. So, tell me about Trey's bad day at work."

"Most of the days are good," began Trey. "I do like the job and most of the people I work for or with. Even this Damndemic schedule of alternating between office and home has been tolerable. Well, I told you I am a financial analysis for the bank. As we are international, my supervisor had me do a detailed analysis of India's twenty best investments. I worked for three weeks on that thing."

"What happened?" interjected Felicia. "Didn't they like the report?"

"They loved the report! The thing is that my supervisor put her name on it. She didn't even acknowledge the work I did in a meeting we had. I know this might only be my ego being bruised, but I feel like I got punched in the gut. Also, I don't know what to do about it."

"That's tough," sympathized Felicia. "It totally sucks when you work hard at something, and someone else takes the credit. It's okay to feel a little beat up by something like that."

"Are you giving me permission to feel miserable?" inquired Trey.

"Yes, but only for another ten minutes or so. Unfortunately, I've gone through this kind of thing too. There are lessons you will learn from it. They are good to keep in mind, too, because as sure as the sun rises again tomorrow, it will happen again."

"That's reassuring," said Trey sarcastically. "So, what happened to you?"

It was Felicia's turn to stop and think. "Hmmm, I have had too many similar things happen to me but let me give you two of them. The first was when I worked for another college. I wasn't the department chair then. The one there had recently announced her retirement and was taking the last of her accumulated vacation time, which was something like two months."

"You were the acting head?" asked Trey.

"Not officially, but it fell on me by default. I thought that wasn't a bad thing because I applied for the position. Anyway, we had a huge budget issue to arise. I won't bore you with the details, but I worked something like 80 hours a week for two weeks straight on it to fix things. I did some rather creative work, and I solved the problem. As things went, not only didn't I get a pat on the back, but I never did get the promotion to the department head. That's the reason why I am at the university I am now."

"That's crazy! You didn't even get thanked, and you put all that work into it. You do know how I feel, then," said Trey.

"Definitely! As for someone taking credit for your work, I worked at a company while in college. They gave me the assignment to write a company newsletter to be distributed within the company and to customers. I did some diligent research and brought together the company's history while tying it to future goals. I have to say I liked what I did. I got it done by the deadline and sent it to my supervisor. I couldn't wait to hear what he had to say. Well, I waited, and I waited. The first I heard anything about it was when I received the newsletter! It was all my words, and his name was on it."

Trey exclaimed, "Ouch! You do get how my day went. Did you ever say anything to your supervisor?"

"No, I was young. I alternated between crying and wanting to rip off his head. I compromised by doing nothing."

"I think I'm too old to cry," said Trey, "though ripping off my boss' head entered my mind today. Driving home, I found myself asking if I was overreacting, or does everything seem worse because of the Damndemic?"

Felicia said, "At least you had the presence of mind to ask some insightful questions. Did you get any answers?"

"Hey, I did the questions; you can do the answering, Felicia. You sound like you have had more of this type of thing than me."

"Not something I want to be known for," said Felicia, "but I have learned some things from my experiences that I have found helpful. You want to hear them?"

"Go for it. I'm all for my lousy day to be a learning experience."

Felicia took a deep breath. "You've heard me use this word before, but it comes down to mindfulness. When we are truly mindful, you look at a person or a situation in a very non-judgmental way. I will be the first to say that this is a skill we have to develop and practice. Part of human nature is judging things, whether it is something we should be doing or not. Furthermore, unless you are a total narcissist, the person we tend to judge the most is ourselves. With all this judging going on, it becomes difficult to look at what we are going through objectively."

Trey had a questioning look on his face. "Why is objectivity important?"

"Because then you can see the entire picture without anything biasing your thought process. When scientists do research, they try to do their experiment in as much of a pristine environment as possible so that they can better evaluate their results. When you get rid of your judging filters, you have a clearer look at a person or situation."

"Okay, I understand that concept," said Trey, "but I'm not taking out my feelings about what I am going through, am I?"

"No, not at all," Felicia said quickly. "In fact, once you drop the judging, you can examine your feelings with a calmer eye. You can figure out how and why you feel as you do. Often when someone is dealing with an issue, they can be all worked up inside. The first thing to do is decide if you are feeling frustrated or mad or sad or whatever. Mindfulness requires the ability to be aware of all your senses and how you interpret them.

14

"As you practice mindfulness more, you get better at figuring out your reactions to emotion. That's important because you will get better at controlling your reactions. We often have a knee-jerk reaction to certain emotions. The good ones like smiling when receiving a compliment or easily acknowledging an act of kindness are no-brainers, and they are good ones. Where we get into trouble is if we yell back if someone yells at us. It is particularly an issue if our boss is doing the yelling."

Trey grinned. "I tend not to do that, though I wanted to do it today."

Felicia responded, "I certainly understand why, but it was good you understand that it is something you wanted to do, but you had the self-control not to give in to your instincts. Mindfulness helps protect us from doing anything hasty. Now that you avoided doing anything rash, you have given yourself the time to closely examine the situation. You can think better about any people involved and how they contributed to the issue."

"I have to say that I'm feeling calmer just with you walking me through this process. Is this how it works for you?" asked Trey.

"It does, and it didn't take me all that long for exercising mindfulness to turn it into a part of my life. It became a good habit that I fall back to in so many circumstances. You have now taken the judging and emotion out of the equation and can look at everything more objectively and make some smart decisions regarding your next course of action. I'll tell you right now, sometimes that course of action might be to do nothing."

"That's a solution?" exclaimed Trey.

"Let us look at what happened today. You are fairly new there at the bank. I don't know what your relationship is like with your supervisor, but I am sure nothing good would have come out of storming in her office and loudly complaining about what she did to you."

"You're right about that. I'm not even sure if I could have a quiet conversation about how I felt with what happened," sighed Trey.

"If you can talk to her, even if it is down the road, I believe that communication is always best. However, if you can't, you can't. So, what other option do you have?"

Trey sat back in his chair and looked off in the distance. Refocusing on Felicia, he said tentatively, "Make sure it doesn't happen again?"

"Ding, ding, ding! We have a winner," shouted Felicia. Lowering her voice, she continued. "I learned from my experience with the newsletter incident. Whenever I did something for a supervisor, I copied everyone I could think of with my work. That way, supervisors, managers, bosses, and colleagues all knew the work I did. I have to say I never had anyone try to take credit for my work again."

"Wow, such a simple idea, but brilliant. I like it," said Trey.

"That's what mindfulness brings you. It gives you the clarity to examine your problem. More often than not, the way to alleviate any similar issue in the future tends to be simple and straightforward. When we are in the middle of a problem, though, we don't always see that."

"I can see that. I'm going to look at today again and use your mindfulness technique."

"Some events are going to make you try and use mindfulness on steroids," said Felicia. "Look at this entire Damndemic thing. We are facing issues because of it, but many more people have it even harder. You know, today is a good reminder that we always must practice mindfulness. With the Damndemic, many people are trying to do what they need to do to stay healthy or keep their career going. Unfortunately, they keep running into walls. It shows why you have to stay present in the moment and train yourself to think and analyze problems clearly. Mindfulness gives us that."

"I hear the front door opening," said Trey, "and it is going to get crazy in here in a minute. Thank you so much for what you said today. Tell you what – as we keep fighting through the Damndemic, let's be there for each other to be present in the moment, listen to each other, and think through any issues we face. I want to get better at this mindfulness. I see it being useful for so much even being a husband and father."

"You're pretty brilliant yourself, Trey. I'm glad you see all the benefits of mindfulness. I'm sure we'll talk about it more, but it helps when you have an accountability partner for something like practicing mindfulness. It helps both of us. I like it!"

"Okay, Felicia, stay safe out there and wear your mask. I'll talk to you later."

Courageous Reflections

Now that you have read "Mindfulness on Steroids":

- What resonated with you?

- What caused you to think and ponder?

- What made you curious to investigate further?

- What notes could you jot down?

- Has the Damndemic made you more aware of practicing mindfulness in your day-to-day life?

- We/you are only in control of implementing mindfulness in your life. How are you responding?

- What action(s)/goal(s) could you take to experience the best outcome of mindfulness in your professional life, personal life, and dealing with the Damndemic?

- What is your plan, and when do you start, and how will you know when you have achieved your goals?

Reflection Notes

_____

_____

_____

_____

_____

_____

_____

_____

_____

_____

_____

_____

_____

_____

_____

_____

_____

_____

_____

_____

Chapter 3
Dilemma Across the Generations
#generations

Trey was laughing so hard that tears were coming out of his eyes. "I can't believe you said that to him. And he just left?"

"Yeah," said Felicia. "How a pharmaceutical sales rep mistook me for a doctor and wouldn't stop trying to sell his wares to me, I have no idea. It was the first time I was in the office for two weeks. I know my office is across from the campus clinic, but all the buildings and offices are clearly marked."

"I didn't have anything that funny happen to me this past week. Though my supervisor had to go to Europe for a few meetings and she is in quarantine because one of the countries told her she had to go there since she was from the United States. Wherever she is at has terrible cell and internet service, so she doesn't contact the office much. Those of us in her department have been enjoying it."

Felicia gave her friend scolding looks over the video screen. "I am surprised you are enjoying her misfortune."

"Hey, I'm new with this international business, but if I was planning on going to another country during the Damndemic, I would certainly be reading up on any issues or restrictions before I get there."

"Smart man. Hey, I have a situation at work I wanted to run by you. Do you still have a few minutes?"

"Sure, but it is my turn to make dinner. You got 15 minutes," said Trey.

Felicia said, "Alyse has it good; she doesn't have to cook dinner every night. Since the Damndemic I have done more cooking and baking for myself. I added another half hour to my work out every day, so I don't gain the COVID 19 pounds. Anyway, I have noticed something interesting since the Damndemic started."

"What's that? Most people don't know how to wear their masks properly?" asked Trey.

"That too, but that's not what I want to discuss. I'm not sure if I have more time to observe people because of using video conferencing so much, but there is a difference with how the generations communicate."

Trey gave her a deadpan look for 30 seconds before saying, "You are just noticing that now? I have two kids under 10 who make me feel like 90 whenever we have a conversation. I don't know how to tell you this, Felicia, but that has been the way of the world since the first parents had children."

"I'm not talking about children here," explained Felicia. "Though they are young and sometimes act like kids. I'm mainly talking about millennials."

"Oh right, we only miss being classified as one by a little bit," said Trey. "At least the older ones are almost our age. So, what's the problem? Don't they do what they are told?"

"They respond to direction and meet their responsibilities okay, but they have a different work ethic and values than we do."

Trey asked, "Did something happen recently to trigger this, Felicia. You get along with everybody. I know you work with everyone from 18-year-old student interns to professors who were personal friends with Einstein."

Felicia said, "It wasn't so much something happened as a discussion I had at a staff meeting. We are launching a capital campaign in two years, and we've started the planning. I said I wanted a comprehensive section in the materials on the history of the university. I was hit with two of my staff saying, 'Why?' I was a little taken aback. It seemed like a no-brainer to me. If you are going to people, mainly alumni, to give big bucks to the college, you want them to embrace all the school has done since its inception."

Trey chuckled, and Felicia looked at him crossly. Before she could say anything, he held up his hand and said, "Wait. I'm not laughing at you. Let me guess what happened next. You probably gave a very well-constructed answer on the reason why the history of the school was important, and you were met with blank looks."

Now, Felicia looked at him suspiciously. "You been ghost-bombing my Zoom calls?" she asked.

"No, I have run into that type of attitude when I talk or interact with millennials. I also have similar issues, but most of mine occur with those older than me. You know, the late Baby Boomers or those older. Remember, I work in banking. It is an industry that still has many older people near the top."

"How is that related to what I ran into?" asked Felicia. You're talking about issues across generations."

"Exactly!" exclaimed Trey. "I don't think you have a generational problem. When we first met at that conference years ago, do you remember what you told me is the key to everything, whether it was at work, school, dating, etc."

Felicia didn't even have to think about it. "Communication."

"Correct. The thing I have come to appreciate is that one size doesn't fit all when you communicate with someone. In this context, I'm talking about issues between different age groups. You know how I arrived at this insight?"

"How?" asked Felicia with a smile, feeding him the next line.

"In a bar, watching the Chicago Bears play Monday night football with a couple of buddies. I was in there wearing my Gale Sayers jersey that my uncle gave me. To explain, Sayers was a fantastic running back in the 60s and my father's favorite player. I wasn't even born then, but before my brothers and sister could sit down to eat when my uncle was over, he'd ask us Chicago Bear questions during football season or Cubs' stuff when it was time for baseball. Anyway, I got to know the whole history of the Chicago Bears and football, in general.

"Getting back to the bar, we were at one table and a group of millennials were at the other. One guy said he didn't remember a guy named Sayers on the team. As I explained who he was, it led to a discussion that went on all night about the history of the Bears. They were fans, but they didn't care about the past. All that mattered to them was what the Bears did in the coming year."

Felicia looked at Trey with a very skeptical look. "Your entire theory about communication between generations is based on that?"

"Of course not, but it did make me curious. Whenever I got in with a group of people with millennials present, I would pick their brain on an entire range of subjects. It was interesting what I found. There were no good movies before 1980, let alone the black and white ones, which were truly ancient. Football didn't exist before Madden was a video game. Supply and demand were an old economic term from sometime during the Roman Empire, and there was never a good politician in Washington unless it was Bernie Sanders."

"That sounded a little like my discussion at the staff meeting," said Felicia.

"The point I have derived from my non-scientific research is that millennials don't have any respect or much knowledge of history in almost any category you want to pick. They are all about the here and now. It boils down to what is trending across social media, and anything more than a year or two old is not in that category."

"That can't be true of all of them," said Felicia in surprise.

"No, but I haven't seen much to dispute the generalization. Of course, there are exceptions. Whenever I talk to millennials about important subjects and they don't know what our country did in the world before 9/11, I always think of that old saying, 'Those who do not know history are doomed to repeat it.' It is a frightening prospect."

"I'll say," responded Felicia. "Hate to think of those mistakes out there that will be repeated from ignorance. So, how do you change their attitude or outlook on history?"

"Way above our pay grade," replied Trey. "However, I have learned from my social research that when you need to communicate with a millennial, you have to do it in a way that will resonate with them."

Felicia said sarcastically, "You mean with a text message."

"You think you are kidding, but that is exactly what you have to do," said Trey.

Felicia's shoulders sagged. "I really thought I was kidding. On the other hand, it is pretty easy to do. Excuse me if I'm a little skeptical about this."

Felicia could see Trey tapping his pencil as he thought about what he wanted to say. He started with, "Remember a couple Zooms ago you schooled me in mindfulness? Well, apply that to this situation. If you look at the issue in a nonjudgmental manner, the issue is getting your information through to your millennials. Now you could sit them down and lecture them on history or get them books on why history is important. Do you think that will work?"

"No, I will be met with glazed eyes or disgruntled mumblings about not reading a book since school," said Felicia.

"You know your audience. What you need to do is a little research on your part to find information that they will look at on the subject. That means videos, podcasts, or anything on a social media outlet that their age group uses. It is not that they aren't opened to learn new things, but you have to meet them where they are. You don't want to compromise on the point you want to make, so you need to find a way to give them information they will respond to in a positive manner."

Felicia was nodding at Trey's words. "And here I thought I was a great communicator," she said.

"You are, in my opinion," said Trey. "I have come to realize that we have to be more inventive in the manner we use to communicate. As I said before, one size doesn't fit all."

Felicia asked, "Have you put your knowledge to use?"

"I didn't plan it, but I did with a project I did at work. For some analysis I was doing, I figure it would be helpful doing an employee survey to get different perceptions of what the financial markets will be doing in the next five years. I sent out an email to a hundred people. All those who are around our age or early baby boomers responded very quickly. I got a couple responses from those who were older or younger, but not many. I thought about resending the email to those who didn't respond, but I thought better of it."

"What did you end up doing?" asked Felicia.

"I kept the survey intact, but I adapted it to be delivered in different methods. For the older staff, I did it in letter form and sent it out in snail mail. For the millennial crowd, I sent it as a link on a text message. For anyone I missed, I posted it on the part of the company website under the staff section. In the end, I had a 95% return rate, and I must attribute it to sending the survey out in ways I thought specific generations would respond. It wasn't very scientific, and I only used three methods. The website idea was only a catch-all for anyone who didn't respond to anything else."

"Trey, you might qualify as a sociologist doing those type of experiments," Felicia said with a laugh.

"Thanks, but it was more about being inventive due to desperation, but now I know how to target my approach to individuals in the company depending on their age range. It does save some frustration."

"I can see how mindfulness came into play with the problem. You were able to easily focus on a solution based on the issue of communicating effectively. Trying to get the millennials and the younger generations after them to think like we do is too big of a problem."

"Let's face it, Felicia, it is an impossible problem. What did your parents think of the music you liked when you were 20?"

"They didn't think much of it."

"How do you feel about music your millennials listen to?"

"What I've heard, I don't think much of it."

Trey said, "There you have the circle of life as it has been forever. My son showed me something on TikTok the other day. I had to ask what TikTok was. We came of age when technology seemed to be giving us 100 new things a day. We believe we are so up to date on all that is out there. Well, my dear, tech now seems to be giving birth to 1000 new things a day and we aren't as sophisticated as we thought. The generation below us, however, lives with this stuff 24/7."

Felicia sat back in her chair and tented her hands below her face. She leaned her chin on the points of her fingers looking very thoughtful. "You know, Trey, I feel like you unlocked a door I didn't even know was closed. Thinking back on the past few years of working, I can understand your point. It is almost like, if you can't beat them, join them."

"You don't need to go join the other side, but you can communicate with them more easily. A wise woman once told me that was a good 75% of any problem that needed solving."

Felicia laughed at that one. "So, the student has turned into the teacher?" she asked.

"That's another circle of life thing. I hope it helps. You might not get your millennials to fully appreciate the importance of history, but they might learn something about it."

"Sometimes I think all this tech and communication ability we have is a two-edged sword," stated Felicia.

"Why?" asked Trey.

"Because we have access to almost anything we want, and a lot we don't want, at the touch of a button. With all this capability, it overloads our brains. We naturally drift to what interests us. It's like there is plenty of dessert out there, so why bother with the vegetables. I can see how my millennials get so focused on only what they enjoy or believe. There is almost no room for anything else."

Trey said, "On the other hand, we were able to binge-watch whatever we wanted when the Damndemic started. It isn't all bad."

"No, not bad at all," said Felicia. "However, I can see where all our tech is a consideration when you are trying to communicate with others."

Courageous Reflections

Now that you have read "Dilemma Across the Generations":

- What resonated with you?

- What caused you to think and ponder?

- What made you curious to investigate further?

- What notes could you jot down?

- Have you ever run into issues with communicating with someone who is of a different generation than you are in your day-to-day life?

- We are in control of how we communicate with others. How are you responding?

- What action(s)/goal(s) could you take to experience the best outcome of communicating in your professional life, personal life, and dealing with the Damndemic?

- What is your plan, and when do you start, and how will you know when you have achieved your goals?

Reflection Notes

_____

_____

_____

_____

_____

_____

_____

_____

_____

_____

_____

_____

_____

_____

_____

_____

_____

_____

_____

_____

Chapter 4
Self-Preservation vs. the Right Thing to Do
#BLM

L eaning his head against the door, Trey took a deep breath and then opened it. He braced himself for the evitable assault of Trevor and Kim, racing to see who could hug him first. Trey said, "Umph," as he took the impact of his two children. He hugged them extra tight as his wife, Alyse, came in and kissed him. She could immediately see something was wrong.

"Oh, Trey, did you think what would happen did?" she asked.

"Yeah, Babe, I'm afraid so. It was like seeing a tidal wave about to hit me, and I couldn't do a damn thing about it. I'm now a member of the unemployed." Looking at the concern on her face, he quickly added, "Don't worry, we have enough in savings for a while, and I have places interested in me. Even with this Damndemic going on, we'll be fine."

Alyse smiled, "Your name for this thing has caught on. That's how I refer to it all the time. Aren't you supposed to have your Zoom thing with Felicia today?"

"Yes, but I can easily cancel it. She'll understand," Trey said.

"No, don't do that. She's good to talk with. I called her the other day because of some stuff going on at where I work. Felicia is great to bounce off that sort of thing. Besides, I'm in the middle of making dinner. I'll keep the kids out there with me."

Trey went into the room he and his wife designated as their office and flopped back in his chair. Trying to put on a brave face, he fired up the laptop

29

and went to his email for the Zoom invitation Felicia sent out every week. Seeing he was right on time, Trey clicked on the link and waited for Felicia to come on the screen.

"Hi there," Felicia said with a grin. Almost instantly, she took on a more serious look. "Oh no, what happened?"

"It's that obvious?" Trey asked.

"As clear as if I was sitting right next to you," said Felicia.

"I got fired," Trey said simply.

"What the hell for?" asked Felicia. "It sounded like you were doing so well at the bank."

"That's the irony of the situation. I was. Almost everyone liked the work I did, and I got along personally with my colleagues."

"You said "almost" about people liking what you did. Why do I think there is someone there who was a fly in the ointment?"

"My supervisor," said Trey with a touch of disgust.

"The one who took credit for your work that time?" asked Felicia.

"Yes, but I only told you about the one time. There were others. I finally brought it up to her at a performance review. I was very professional and didn't dwell on it, but I think that sealed my fate."

"Really! She terminated you for that!" exclaimed Felicia.

"I think so. The official reason was because she said I didn't do something I was supposed to do. The thing is, she never told me it was my assignment. I had no clue. As it was, I only found out from someone at my supervisor's level in the company that is what went down. She screwed up and wasn't going to take the rap. So, she blamed the low man on the totem pole that she wasn't too crazy about at all. That would be me!"

Trey could see Felicia's eyes begin to water. "Hey, don't let that get to you.". Trey replied, "I'll be fine. Honestly, there were many things about this job that I did not like."

"You got paid very well there," said Felicia.

"Okay, the money I'll miss," said Trey with a laugh. "This is probably a good thing. I found out I don't like my most personal relationship at work being with my laptop and spreadsheets. I did miss interacting with people more. The thing is, I worked hard when I applied for that job. I had stellar references from colleagues, aced an incredibly involved interview process, and thought I had my dream job. Today, it turned into a nightmare."

"You know, I heard something similar occurred in the Science Department here at the university. Somebody was let go, and the impression was that she had to 'take one for the team.' It was all because a tenured professor had totally screwed up a relationship with a university's prominent donor. I had no say in the situation, but it sounded unfair how it went down for the staff person fired. I know some internal investigation is going on, but who knows if anything will come of it." Trey could see her shrugging on the screen. "You have a lawsuit situation there with what your supervisor did to you?"

It was Trey's turn to shrug. "They have a lot of money for lawyers, and I don't. Even though they terminated me, I'm supposed to get some severance package. I'll see what that looks like. I think I'm getting it because some of the higher-ups know what happened wasn't right. Can you explain to me why upper management knows this is wrong, but they are still going along with it?" asked Trey.

Felicia picked up a pen and started tapping it on the table as she thought. Stopping, she looked directly at Trey and said, "I can give you a bunch of management theory to explain it all, but it comes down to people being people and organizations not wanting to go off the rails. While it is commendable and proper to say, 'My bad,' when we screw up, there are many people who can never get those words out of their mouth or utter the sentence, 'I'm sorry.' If you are a supervisor, you should not want those kinds of people working for you because they will inevitably lead to trouble and contention. The truth is that no matter the standards a company broadcasts that it adheres to regarding the type of people they employ, there are always many exceptions that go under the radar because those not doing their job are experts at deflecting and end up getting promoted. I've seen it."

"What have you personally seen or experienced?" asked Trey.

"I have seen people move up in the universities I have served when they fail to complete routine tasks like answering their emails. If they are given an assignment requiring their attention and don't do it, they would say nobody ever trained them properly. Another trick along those lines was that if they got a job they didn't want to do, they convened a group meeting to complete the task. My personal favorite, and I had to terminate someone for pulling this one, is when a report is late. Instead of just telling me and asking for more time, this person had an underling copy and paste someone else's report together and replace the primary names. I saw through that one right away. I was so mad. I waited two days to terminate that employee because I was so angry. I wanted to be professional when I told him why I was firing him. It took me those extra days to get rid of the rage."

"What would you have done if he came to you admitting that he wasn't ready with his report?" Trey asked.

"I try to use those moments as learning opportunities," said Felicia. "When you manage others, you have a responsibility to help them get better. A bad supervisor cringes if one of his or her people moves up the ladder to a better position. A good supervisor embraces and celebrates those moments."

"That's some good insight there I didn't realize," said Trey. "When I was going after my Ph.D. and working at the college, my supervisor was Ms. Greene. She was African American like me. At first, I thought she might be a little easier on me because of that, but it seemed like it was the opposite. She would give me many compliments in private, such as telling me that people appreciated my honesty, integrity, and being authentic. However, she also coached me to keep a foot on the throat of my subordinates, and she rarely gave my department or me any public recognition."

"Sounds like she was a supervisor that believed in tough love," said Felicia.

"She certainly was," responded Trey. "Whenever I asked her why she was so hard on me, she would reply, 'I want you to be better.' I guess it worked, because my colleagues, subordinates, and the students often told me that they were impressed with my work."

"Anyone in a position of supervising others develops their own style of working with people. A good supervisor knows that it is necessary to know how to talk with those under them. It shouldn't be one style used on everyone. I hope this Ms. Greene could see that this was the style that would get the most out of you. She might work with someone else completely different. It takes work to be a good supervisor."

Trey said, "You mentioned earlier something about companies not wanting to go off the rails when a supervisor gets rid of an employee with great potential, and, yes, I am talking about I'm here. Why wouldn't my bank back me instead of my witch of a supervisor."

"That's extremely complicated without knowing all the dynamics between the witch and the bank. I'm sure she has been there for a time while you are rather new. Like it or not, longevity factors into decision-making about personnel. Sometimes it goes the other way, and a company rather keep the new person if they consider someone who has been around for a long time as dead wood. It depends on the company culture. You would hope that the powers-that-be are an enlightened bunch, but the deciding factors are as simple as who gives the company a better shot at a profit, or who you dismiss or promote leads to the least distractions."

"You mean I have to put up with this crap the rest of my career?" asked Trey incredulously.

"Buckle up, buttercup," said Felicia. "It is pretty widespread. As you look for a new job somewhere, do your due diligence in checking out the company's culture. If they believe in constant leadership and management training, the odds will be better that everyone working there has good common sense and exercises people skills. And when you get the opportunity to further your skillset with managing people, practice them all the time to become more natural at using them. I mean, I know you are a good people person, but we all need to refine our skills constantly."

"Any other tips?" asked Trey.

"What you experienced with your supervisor has a name. It is called imposter syndrome. I'm sure you can identify others acting like that with some behaviors or characteristics you have observed," stated Felicia.

"I can think of a few," said Trey. "Someone in that imposter syndrome is definitely a phony. They probably like to use that bogus term, 'alternate facts.'"

"Good point," said Felicia. "They are frauds, and they know it deep down. This brings their lack of self-esteem to the surface. Often that translates into a controlling individual who wants everything to happen his or her way. If they are ever questioned about any of their work, they immediately get defensive."

"I have also seen, at least with the witch, she was very manipulative of all of us in her department. She also wasn't above lying and denying anything wrong with how she conducted business." Trey stopped for a second. "The more we are talking, the happier I am that I am out of there. I hate to say this, but there was a bit of racism in her too. I don't know; maybe bias is a better word. She is an Indian woman, and it seemed like she was always harder on anyone not of that heritage."

"She could very well be micro-racist. It happens no matter someone's race. I'm not sure if we will ever eliminate that completely," said Felicia sadly.

"Felicia, thank you so much for talking me through this. I do feel better. I'm going to enjoy a few days off and tackle my job-hunting on Monday. I think I need the mental rest."

"Nothing wrong with that," said Felicia. "Do you have prospects?"

"I do, which is one reason I'm only upset, not devastated. Do you have a minute for something else that came to mind while we were talking? It's sort of related."

"Of course! Tell me about it," said Felicia.

"I got to thinking about that video where the cops are kneeling on George Floyd and slowly choking him to death. You listen to what is going on in Minnesota about this case, and it made me wonder if people in the workplace take the idea of self-preservation at all costs too far. Here it isn't only affecting someone's livelihood; it caused a death. The police insist they were acting properly."

Felicia looked glum. "It has been going on for too long, Trey. We have seen it with the police for years. Politicians are great at self-preservation; some have raised it to an art form. You know, if someone's actions at work lead to death, it becomes the ultimate self-preservation time. Again, it is not something we can get away from, but every industry can do their best at training people to avoid such occurrences."

"We have a long way to go," said Trey. "I think this Damndemic only heightens the issue of taking personal responsibility. It seems to be something that has gone by the wayside. I remember when my uncle used to say that the only thing you can hang onto is keeping your word and having a good name. It appears that this has gone by the wayside."

"Well, my friend, it shows that just because something is old school, it doesn't mean it is obsolete," finished Felicia.

Courageous Reflections

Now that you have read "Self-Preservation vs. the Right Thing to Do":

- What resonated with you?

- What caused you to think and ponder?

- What made you curious to investigate further?

- What notes could you jot down?

- What are descriptions from your observations in life when you hear imposter syndrome?

- How do you respond when faced with imposter syndrome from someone?

- What action(s)/goal(s) could you take to experience the best outcome of dealing with imposter syndrome in your professional life, personal life, and dealing with the Damndemic?

- What is your plan, and when do you start, and how will you know when you have achieved your goals?

Reflection Notes

_____

_____

_____

_____

_____

_____

_____

_____

_____

_____

_____

_____

_____

_____

_____

_____

_____

_____

_____

_____

Chapter 5
Ambushed by Thieves
#metoo

T he kettle finally started to whistle on the stove. Felicia went over and picked it up with almost a violent motion and poured hot water into the mug holding the chamomile tea bag. She thought hard about what she wanted to drink after her Zoom meeting was over with the Board's finance committee for her university. She was ready to spit nails from her anger but decided wine wasn't a good idea at the moment. Instead, she went for a calming mug of tea. As she finished pouring the water, she thought that she needed a whole jug of tea to calm down.

She held up the mug and sniffed in the aroma. The warm steam waffled over her nose, and she felt a little calmer just breathing in the tea. She took a hot sip and looked out the window. The day had been gray and rainy all day, and it pretty much matched her mood. She paced around her kitchen and wondered what to do about the mess presented to her at the meeting. She was thankful it was a video conference, or she might have had a messy confrontation with the university's CFO.

Felicia's position at the school had her responsible for bringing in general donations to the university and managing the entire endowment program. At any time, she or her staff were asking for money for a capital campaign, a particular project, or to put it into the school's endowment account. She answered to the CFO, and there were never any problems until now. Of course, she never did such a detailed review of the school's accounting process before this meeting. What she saw sickened her, and now she had to figure the best way to handle it.

She stopped thinking about it as the dinging of the computer announced someone was on Zoom. She knew Trey was responding to the weekly invite, so she hurried over to begin their talk.

"You look mad," Trey started out saying. "I sure hope it's not at me."

Felicia tried a smile but failed miserably. "I had a rough day, to say the least. I'll tell you all about it in a minute. First, please tell me how you are doing. Any employment prospects?"

"I have some good news on that score. The University of Chicago and I are meeting again tomorrow about a position they are creating. It combines some teaching and doing economic analysis. I'd be using MBA and doctoral students to help me spearhead a program that the school wants to sell to other financial organizations. I am to raise their profile through publishing and things of that sort."

"Meeting again sounds like a positive," said Felicia.

"Honestly, it is all about nailing down the details. I think when we make some decisions tomorrow, they will offer it to me," said Trey with a smile he didn't even try to hide.

"Trey, that's great. What did you think of the people you met there?" asked Felicia.

"That's the weird thing about the whole process. I haven't set foot on the campus yet. We did everything through phone calls and videoconferencing. It's the new Damndemic way of conducting business, I guess, but I liked everyone that was part of the interview."

Felicia managed a genuine chuckle. "I tell those out of work or looking for something new that it is possible to get one during the Damndemic. Now, I have you to point to as a sterling example."

No, no, no," said Trey quickly. "Don't use me as an example for anything until I sign on the dotted line."

"No worries," said Felicia, making a zipping motion across her lips, "but you better text me as soon as you get it."

"I promise," said Trey, holding up his right hand as if taking an oath. "Now, what's going on with you?"

Felicia picked up her mug and took a long drink. She set it back down as she said, "My Chief Financial Officer at the university is doing some funny things with money, and I don't know what to do about it. I know I have to report it because I'm not going to go down for something I didn't do, but it isn't going to be easy."

Trey said, "That's big stuff, Felicia. How did you find out about it?"

"The Board of Directors decided last year that the university would do an internal audit of everything. I'm talking about the programs in all the different schools, the sports programs, recruiting new students, etc. You name it, and each department needed to do a full program and financial audit of its respective responsibilities. If we find anything to be way out of sync, an outside firm will do an external audit. The Board wanted to ensure we are doing everything as efficiently and properly as possible. It was their way of not raising tuition more. They hoped we would find some ways to improve what we do without costing more money."

Trey nodded. "That's a great idea. Works better than throwing money at things without thinking it through. Not many institutions try to do such house cleaning."

"Of course, nobody, including me, was incredibly happy about doing it. It is a lot of work on top of what we already do, but I spent a lot of time pulling things together in my department and parceling out some of the work to my staff. I was a little behind on the project until we had the Damndemic. Then I found myself with some blessed uninterrupted time and plowed through a great deal of information, including financials related to my department. That's when I found the issue."

"Was money or something missing?" asked Trey.

"Sort of," answered Felicia. "Many people give to the university. Many donations and programs we conduct have the money go into the general account. The school uses it for whatever they want based on the budget. However, we also receive many contributions where the donor earmarks the money for something specific – a building, a program, something for the football team, whatever. To make the story short, I found money earmarked for specific items, and it wasn't going to them. Not only could a donor call 'fraud' on us, but we would never see another dime from him or her in the future."

"I can see the problem with what you found," said Trey. "I'd be ticked off if I gave to some organization, and they didn't use my money for what I asked."

"You got that right," said Felicia. "My dilemma is twofold. How do I blow the whistle and go up against the CFO? Second, how do I do it so that the situation is treated low-key enough that the university doesn't get blown out of the water with bad publicity?"

"You put my three weeks of unemployment in perspective. It wasn't really that bad compared to what you are facing. How did you find out this was going on?" asked Trey.

"Part of the audit meant going through our financial records with a fine-tooth comb. I'm very well-versed in reading the reports about what my department brings in, but I never had any reason to look at how the money gets spent because that isn't my circus. The audit forced me to do it. As I caught on how to read the details, I saw money raised for particular projects had a portion of the money going into the general fund, usually for university payroll. As I learned more about our system, I saw that it took a deliberate accounting transaction to move money like this; it wasn't an accident."

"Did you bring this up to anyone?" asked Trey.

"I finished up a meeting about an hour ago, and I presented my findings. If we weren't on Zoom, I think the CFO would have shot real daggers at me with his eyes. I shared a bunch of documents with everyone on the call, showing what I had found. The bottom line is that money went into the general fund quite often when it wasn't supposed to occur at all. When I asked what was going on, the CFO was deathly quiet for almost a full minute. He tried to look like he was looking at what was on the screen, but he was seething."

Trey sat back in his chair and shook his head. "Let me get this straight. You blew the whistle to someone who probably knows exactly what's going on, if not making it occur by his hand. How does this go from here for you?"

"Well, I might have miscalculated how to handle this," said Felicia sheepishly. "I think I went into today's meeting thinking there was a logical reason for the moving around of money. I think I surprised the CFO so much with my findings that he didn't know what to say. Finally, he blurted out something about one of his staff had looked at the same records, and there was a different explanation for it."

"What was the explanation?" asked Trey.

Felicia threw her hands up in the air. "I have no idea. He terminated the conference call soon after that, saying we had run through the allotted time. I could tell from the faces of a few of the other department heads that they too would have liked to hear the answer."

"You know what this means?" said Trey.

"That the CFO is doing something right now to make it all okay," said Felicia. "You can answer this better than me, but isn't it hard to hide something in a complex accounting system after the fact of something being done?"

"Depending on what your accounting software is, it is tough to do. Most systems make it impossible to erase a transaction. The backups have backups. However, when something is so big as a university your size, it is impossible to run down every discrepancy on a regular audit. The Board audit forced you to look at the minutia. Kudos to you for finding it," said Trey. "I don't have to tell you that you have to work fast on this. What are you going to do?"

"Going by the micro-aggressive signals the CFO was putting out, I have to do something now. The good thing is I have all my data, notes, and suppositions already typed out and ready to go. I needed them for this afternoon's meeting. I think I need to take everything to the university President and Chairman of the Board. After all, the proof is in the numbers. They are in the position to bring in better financial investigators if they believe it is warranted."

"Oh, I have no doubt they think it will be warranted," said Trey. "They have a fiduciary responsibility to the university. They certainly aren't going to want to go down with the ship if something fishy is going on by the CFO. If they happen to be in on it, well, you can cross that speed bump if you come to it. Personally, I always like to deal with one major crisis at a time."

Felicia found she could still laugh after she heard Trey's last line. "I understand what you are saying. I find it hard to believe that my president or anyone on the Board knows what's going on with the donated money. Like me, they are happy to see the total amount continuing to increase. They can ask the CFO about his motivation for what he is doing. That isn't my concern. My first priority is to make sure they understand I had nothing to do with it."

Trey said, "When I was at the bank, we had an entire department devoted to making sure all transactions were conducted properly. We were an international bank, so we had to ensure we were well-informed of every country's banking laws where we had a branch. Nothing gets you in trouble more than the mishandling of money. If that happened by someone in the bank, they rarely got a second chance. I'm sure your CFO knows that. I'm guessing he is sweating bullets right now and sticking pins into his little Felicia doll."

"First, I don't buy into voodoo, and second, it's creepy if he has any doll that looks like me. I know you are joking about that part, but I'm sure you are correct about the sweating. As soon as we wrap up here, I'm going to compose an email to the President and the Chairman and send it off tonight."

"Can I make a suggestion?" asked Trey. "Copy the CFO too. This way, nobody can accuse you of going behind anyone's back, plus you are going to put more pressure on him right away. People tend to make mistakes under stress. Your CFO might do something that brings this to a speedy resolution. Ideally, your accountants can make some legitimate adjustments to make sure that any earmarked money returns to where it belongs."

"Good idea!" exclaimed Felicia. "I wouldn't have thought of that. I certainly don't want to get into a discussion of 'he said, she said. I have too much to do for this to become a long-term problem for me."

Trey added, "You're a good writer. Compose your email so that you say everything without any judgment." He smiled again. "I think you would call it a very mindful letter. Just the facts, ma'am, just the facts."

"I have already been thinking about what to say. Are you busy tonight? Can I send it to you for another set of eyes to read it? You'll let me know if I need to tone it down or if I misuse any of that financial language. You know it better than me."

"That's what friends are for," said Trey. "I think we have said that enough to each other. It is a quiet night, so send it over, and I'll look at it right away. My guess is you'll be taking your CFO by surprise for the second time today."

"This has been a lesson for me," said Felicia. "I always knew I had a financial obligation in my position, but it never occurred to me that I could find something wrong that someone else was doing. If nothing else, this experience will prepare me for it, if it ever happens again, which I fervently hope it never does."

"Hey, you gave me some food for thought," said Trey. "This was a good reminder to pay close attention to my finances and budget in my new position."

"Thanks for the help, Trey. Let me get started on this email. I'll send it over soon. If you can check it and get it back to me right away, I appreciate it. If I don't send it tonight, I'll never sleep."

"Will do," said Trey. "I'm looking forward to receiving it."

Courageous Reflections

Now that you have read "Ambushed by Thieves":

- What resonated with you?

- What caused you to think and ponder?

- What made you curious to investigate further?

- What notes could you jot down?

- Have you ever dealt with financial discrepancy in your business or under your responsibility?

- How do you respond when you find out someone you work with or answer to did something improper?

- What action(s)/goal(s) could you take to experience the best outcome of dealing with financial issues in your professional life, personal life, and dealing with the Damndemic?

- What's your plan, and when do you start, and how will you know when you have achieved your goals?

Reflection Notes

_____

_____

_____

_____

_____

_____

_____

_____

_____

_____

_____

_____

_____

_____

_____

_____

_____

_____

_____

_____

Chapter 6
Making Sense of It All
#sayhername   #saytheirnames

S ometimes after watching the news, Trey felt like he needed a shower. This was one of those times as the news panel on television finished discussing the case of cops shooting another black man. They were speculating what kind of demonstrations would be happening in the city tonight. While his kids didn't pay much attention to the news, they did see things that made them question what was happening in the country.

He had finished his second week at the University of Chicago, and he liked how his new position was going so far. Trey was also grateful that he didn't feel the immense stress he felt toward the end of his time at the bank. Rachel Rodriguez was the person he reported to at the university, and she was the polar opposite of his old boss. Dr. Rodriquez was a renowned economist, and she gave Trey her goals for the new program he was heading. They decided to meet an hour each week to review Trey's progress, with the understanding that those weekly meetings would taper off as Trey became more comfortable in his position.

It seemed that since the Damndemic began, there was more on the news about racism than ever before. Growing up as an African American, Trey was more than a little familiar with racism. He had been in different places and situations where he felt everyone was looking at him because he was black. As he said to Felicia when he lost the bank job, he realized there were some racial overtones with how his supervisor ran her department.

He shut off the television and walked through empty rooms to his office. Trey was glad Alyse was out with the children, and they didn't hear the news while he watched. He felt distraught as he turned on Zoom and started talking with Felicia.

"What's new and exciting this week?" asked Trey.

"My big news is that our CFO quietly resigned. He had been moving money around from what others told me because some of his people had screwed up in receiving money the university was supposed to get from student loans. Somebody didn't do the proper paperwork, and we weren't getting what we should. This was a problem for several years, but nobody caught the issue in time. The CFO said all was in place for proper funds to come into the coffers eventually, and then he would put the money back in the accounts where it belonged."

"Let me see if I understand it. Nobody was actually stealing money, but he was doing the secret reallocation to cover someone's butt," said Trey.

"You got it," Felicia said. "Specifically, the CFO's butt. It was ultimately his responsibility that his people fell down on the job. The thing is he was not doing his job, so it was a problem that kept snowballing."

"So, all is good then?"

Felicia sighed. "Eventually, it will. The necessary transactions are happening internally, and the new CFO's primary responsibility is to clean up the student loan mess. From my point of view, it didn't hurt our reputation, and hopefully, the entire fiasco will stay quiet."

"I'm glad that's over for you," said Trey.

"Me too. How's the University of Chicago treating you so far?" asked Felicia.

"It's all new, but no complaints. Well, maybe one. I have been doing everything remotely. I guess that's the new normal with the COVID Damndemic, but I look forward to getting on campus. Rumor has it I have an office. I want to see it one day."

"I'm sure you will," said Felicia, laughing. "This Damndemic makes me feel like I'm on a hamster wheel sometimes. I keep moving, but don't get anywhere."

"Do you watch more news than before the Damndemic?" asked Trey.

"I watch more TV period than ever in my life," said Felicia. She thought for a moment. "I definitely watch more news. I try not to watch too much. It's too depressing."

"What do you think about all the racial unrest going on in the country?" asked Trey.

"It's terrible. My mother tells me it seems like we went back in time to the 50s or 60s. What brought on this line of questioning?"

"I had the news on before we started our call. There was another black man shot by cops today."

"Oh no, I did not see that" said Felicia. "I understand the anger out there. I get mad, as do many of my friends. With the discussions of systemic racism and more talk about white supremacy, it's also easy to get scared. What makes it even worse is that none of this is new. My Aunt Maria always tells me there isn't anything new under the sun."

"Your aunt sounds like a wise woman," said Trey.

"You don't know the half of it. We talked a few weeks ago, and she went through something pretty intense. She recently finished doing 20 years in the army and retired. She went back to the town she grew up in and hooked up with her old friend Linda. While visiting, Linda's mother asked the two women to pick a few things up for her at the drug store. Linda recently bought a new car and volunteered to drive, so off they went."

"At the drugstore, they divided up the list and went up and down the aisles picking up what they needed. Aunty Maria was at a shelf near the store's front when a gunman ran into the store, threatening the owner. He was robbing the place. When a shot rang out, my aunt ran to where she saw Linda and tackled her to the ground."

"Oh my God!" said Trey. "Were they okay?"

"Yes, nobody got hurt. The owner had a gun under the counter. This wasn't the first time he had an attempted robbery. Not so much for the money but for drugs in the pharmacy area. He put a shot in the ceiling. He figured he could scare the thief, and he was right. He was no more than a kid, and he took off. Now, here is the interesting part. The first cop on the scene was a white guy. The owner is black, and the cop immediately had him surrender his gun and started putting cuffs on him when two other cops came into the store. These cops regularly patrolled the neighborhood and knew the owner. They had their colleague take off the cuffs and made him leave. They said they would take care of everything. They told the other cop to go drive around and see if he could see anyone suspicious around."

"Were the two new cops who came in black?" asked Trey.

"The female cop was of mixed race, and her male partner was white. My aunt gave a statement of what she saw to the white cop. When she told him that she was a decorated army veteran, he thanked her for her service, and she asked him why they came in and took control of the situation and dismissed their fellow cop. He said, 'Liza and I have been patrolling this neighborhood for three years. We know everybody, and they know us. Tom, the owner over there, is good people. We know he keeps a gun here. We also know he has a permit for it. When you know people personally, you don't make assumptions because of their race, gender, or anything else like that.'"

"Okay, that's different than you see in the news," said Trey thoughtfully.

"We don't deal in law enforcement," said Felicia, "but Aunt Maria told me that it gave her hope that some police get the importance of what they are doing. She was happy that these two were in the area. However, she also pointed out the first cop to arrive was a jerk and started assuming things. My aunt said she was getting furious until the other two came in and diffused the situation."

"We need a lot more cops to diffuse situations rather than throwing kerosene on the fires," commented Trey. "George Floyd, Breonna Taylor, and so many more who have needlessly died at the hands of the police are becoming an epidemic. I'm scared now when my kids are out there driving and moving around the city on their own, and I have a few years before that becomes real. Are we going to get better as a country by then?"

"I wish I had an answer, Trey. On my optimistic days, I would say that we will. When I see news stories like you just watched, I fear for the future. That's why anyone who sees the injustice of any action cannot afford to stand in the background. I have friends of all backgrounds who have become more active and vocal than ever before in their lives. It's going to take a lot of people like that to make a difference. We can never quit!"

"I see more people speaking up than ever before, too," said Trey. "However,

I also see and hear about hate groups springing up and being more vocal. It scares the crap out of me sometimes. Alyse started doing our family tree about a year ago. Both of us come from slave families. After the Civil War, both sides of our family went all over the place. I have had sharecroppers, housekeepers, restaurant owners, one jazz musician, and a collection of laborers, blue color workers, doctors, lawyers, and me as a professor in my family. Alyse's family is quite similar. You talk about the so-called American dream, and you can see my family lived it. You cannot start much lower than a slave. It took over 150 years to achieve such lofty goals, but don't people see that many African Americans have pulled themselves up by their bootstraps and didn't have anything handed to them, despite some of the popular rhetoric we hear every day."

"Oh, you mean how minorities are handed everything on a silver platter and never had to work for anything," said Felicia sarcastically.

"Yeah, that's the one," said Trey. "Are people that blind?"

Felicia considered her answer before replying, "No, not everyone is like that. However, those who don't want to acknowledge what black and brown people can do tend to be the loudest and most ignorant. Somehow, we have gotten to the point in America that if you say something long enough and loud enough, it becomes true, even if it isn't. Labeling things 'fake news' and 'alternative facts' allows ignorance to flourish."

Trey saw Felicia pick up a folder on her desk and open it. "I have a question for you, Trey. Are you taking any steps to try and make things better?"

His eyebrows arched as he absorbed what Felicia said. "Me? I think I do what I can. I speak out on what I see wrong. I admit that I don't get into any heavy discussions on social media because I feel like the people I am arguing against aren't going to read what I say. However, if a subject comes up that I feel strongly against, I'll let my opinion be known." He gestured to his laptop. "Even though most of the discussions I end up having these days are on this thing. There have been some lively discussions with family, friends, and colleagues on Zoom conferences."

"That's good," said Felicia. "I certainly have a lot of those too. Let me tell you some of the other things I've started doing the past four years. I've gone out and taken part in protests. The day after President Trump's inauguration, I was out there at the Women's March. I have taken part in candlelight ceremonies honoring people who were shot down. I have encouraged people here at my university to make their voice heard whether they go out or paint a beautiful mural somewhere or take part in a peaceful protest. I have also become prolific writing different representatives on the local, state, and federal levels to actually do something about these problems ripping apart our country. I took a mindful stance not to be an armchair quarterback talking about how things should be in America. I decided to take whatever action I could."

Trey said, "I'm impressed, Felicia. You've certainly given me some food for thought on all of this. I want my kids to have the world a little more equitable when they become adults."

"Then get out there, man. Those years are going to speed by before you know it," said Felicia. "I also realized that there were ways I can help bring about equity here where I work. Sometimes it is taking a stand on the micro-scale of discrimination where you can make a difference. I have started to become more vocal with the university hierarchy when I see something wrong."

"How do you mean?" asked Trey.

Felicia pulled papers from the folder. "I have been systematically calling my bosses out on some things that shouldn't be happening in the way we hire and promote people. It's funny how a public university should be the hallmark of equality, but its institutionalized discrimination has been going on so long that people accept it as a given. Sometimes we have to call people to task for what has been going on before change can set into an organization."

"I never thought of institutionalized discrimination," commented Trey. "What kind of work are you doing along those lines?"

For the last few years, I have been spearheading a movement to change what Human Resources does with staff. Here are four essential items where we are slowly changing the culture of the college. We have stopped offering salaries to new hires above what current long-time employees and staff are making. If the university needs to pay new people more money to come on board, then everyone on that level should be making more."

"Hang on," said Trey, reaching for a pen, "I want to write this down. That's a good one. What else?"

"We are slowly moving nepotism out of hiring. We've had issues with family members of staff who receive preferential treatment with hiring, and then they can't do the job once they are on board. Also, whenever there is a key leadership position available, people of color rarely make the final cut. I have also asked that the HR department report on who they hire so the President, Board, and all department heads are aware of what's going on with our hiring practices. It is starting to make a difference."

"This gives me something to compare with what my new employer is doing," said Trey. "I can see where taking steps like this can be productive."

Felicia said, "While one bold move sometimes results in change, it more often comes about by consistent baby steps that lead toward the larger goal."

Courageous Reflections

Now that you have read "Making Sense of It All":

- What resonated with you?

- What caused you to think and ponder?

- What made you curious to investigate further?

- What notes could you jot down?

- Have you ever dealt with discrimination in your business or under your responsibility?

- How do you respond when confronted with discrimination in any form?

- What action(s)/goal(s) could you take to experience the best outcome of dealing with discrimination issues in your professional life, personal life, and dealing with the Damndemic?

- What's your plan, and when do you start, and how will you know when you have achieved your goals?

Reflection Notes

Chapter 7
The Transition on the Green Pond
#backtonature

Felicia came into her house, frazzled to the max. She didn't get to her campus office much during these days of the Damndemic, but when she did, she felt like she needed to accomplish a week's worth of work in one day. Now, she felt spent. Felicia kicked off her shoes and ran into her bedroom to change into comfy clothes. Before COVID, she liked wearing her business outfits. They didn't feel so comfortable anymore.

Coming back into her living room, Felicia looked at the clock. She knew her Zoom with Trey was today. They had skipped last week's call because he had taken a week away with his family. Now that summer was here, some of the early restrictions of the Damndemic had eased. Felicia had even met two of her friends at a restaurant with outdoor seating last Saturday night. While it seemed weird having people around, it was nice to have a fun time with people she hadn't seen for a while.

Felicia thought how quickly she became conditioned to life in a Damndemic. She now had a collection of masks that she coordinated with what she wore. Truth be told, that was usually an outfit consisting of leggings and a sweatshirt. When she went to the grocery store, she tried to sprint through her shopping. It wasn't comfortable being around a crowd of people. She had felt the anxiety going out to eat on Saturday. It was amazing how a human being could reset what was "normal," depending on the situation.

She missed last week's phone call with Trey. Another thing she noticed about the Damndemic was the immediate realization that she was off her routine whenever something changed in her schedule. In the old days (like five months ago), a routine change would not even register. She found herself smiling as she went over to her laptop and initiated the call.

A very relaxed looking Trey looked back at her with a wave. "Hello, Felicia, how's life treating you today?"

"Not as good as it seems to be treating you. I think you've gotten younger. Does that always happen when you get a week off?" Felicia asked.

"I wish. After these past six months, I decided to relax. As my daughter Kim keeps singing, I decided to 'Let It Go!' It was the best thing I did all year. It was good for all of us, to tell you the truth."

"What did you do?" asked Felicia. "I'm so envious. Tell me everything. At least I can live vicariously through you."

Trey chuckled at that. "You need to go give yourself a break, Felicia. It does wonders for the soul. We split up the week. For the first few days, the entire family went to Alyse's parents' home. We hadn't seen them since Christmas. We all were a little leery with COVID going on, but none of us here had been in contact with anyone who caught the virus, and neither did my in-laws. We agreed to do this only if we formed our own bubble of just us together. Alyse's sister was visiting from California, so it was only seven of us. I love my family, but it was nice to see new faces after being cooped up together with only the four of us."

"I wouldn't know," said Felicia forlornly. "Easter was my family's big gathering, and that was on Zoom. It is getting old."

"After we were there for a few days, we went our separate ways. The grandparents kept the grandkids to spoil them. Alyse and her sister went off to a spa they researched to make sure it was Damndemic safe. I took my backpack and went to a national park along Lake Michigan for a few days of hiking and camping."

Felicia said, "This is a no-brainer for me. I would definitely be with Alyse and her sister. Since when are you a nature boy?"

"Since I was a kid," said Trey. "I grew up in the projects, but our church had a scout troop. I got to love camping and being outdoors. My wife looks at me like I'm crazy, but I find peace in nature that I don't find anywhere else. Since my cellphone still had a strong signal where I was hiking, I shut it off."

"You shut your cellphone off!" yelled Felicia. "What are you, some radical hippie? The audacity of doing such a thing."

Bursting out laughing, it took Trey a minute to get under control. "It is radical, isn't it? It was also a blessing not to feel tethered to anything back in civilization. Now, I did turn it on for a while in the evening to make sure no emergencies were happening and to keep in touch with family, but for the most part, I was off the grid."

"I think I would start to get the shakes if I didn't have my phone," said Felicia. "Let me change that – I know I would. I have run out of here and forgot my phone. I felt naked and vulnerable." She stopped and looked out over the laptop. "That's rather sad, isn't it?"

"I'm not sure about sad, but that is how we become conditioned," said Trey. "The phone has become everyone's security blanket. I know when I'm in the wilderness, or at least what passes for wilderness around here, I get mentally and spiritually lost in what I see. There are no distractions. I ran into a few hikers during my days on the trail, and we would chat a bit at an acceptable social distance. Nobody had a phone to their ear or seemed to care what was going on in the world."

"Right now, you are painting a nice picture of being disconnected from all the craziness going on these days," said Felicia. "How long was this self-imposed retreat?"

"Only three days, but it did wonders for me. I found a beautiful pond to camp by one night. In the twilight, I watched deer and some other animals come down to drink from the water. It was a clear night, and I could lay back and observe the stars, something that I haven't done in ages. I even forgot that I used to like astronomy when I was in high school. I was proud that I could still recognize and find many constellations. When a meteor went streaking across the sky, I felt like it wrapped up the entire night in a bow."

"You and your pond sound like you can give Henry David Thoreau and Walden Pond a run for their money," commented Felicia.

"Nah," said Trey, "I don't write as eloquently. "However, there is a lot to be said to getting away from the hustle and bustle of the world and absorb the quiet. I felt like I did a file cleaning of my hard drive. I can't claim any great insight with my time away, but I feel relaxed and receptive to whatever the world brings my way." Trey gave a rueful grin. "I also know my Zen might be shattered within three days now that I'm back in the real world, but it was nice to give my mind a reset."

"Did Alyse return in the same state of mind?" asked Felicia.

"She did. Part of it was relaxing at the spa and being pampered for a couple of days, but it was more about being with her sister. They are close in age and best friends. It was very therapeutic for them to be together and to talk and have fun together.

"Listening to some people, we have done very well being cooped up at home together with the kids since the Damndemic began, but it is still incredibly stressful. I don't think we realized how much we needed to unwind until we started to do it."

"I live alone, and I feel the stress of it," said Felicia.

"Of course, you do," said Trey. "We have been forced to do things out of most people's comfort zone. Unless you are 100% introverted, nobody is used to being in isolation, whether it is with others or by yourself. I always believed people are social animals. Taking away human contact is cruel and unusual punishment. However, we had to go through these steps to keep others safe."

"Very true," said Felicia thoughtfully. "How did your kids enjoy the time?"

"Other than having them go through grandparent withdrawal when we returned home, they're great. They needed to experience something different too. Now, we'll get back into our regular routine."

Felicia said, "I never thought about the past six months as you paint them. Even though how we are living seems normal now, it so different than what life was. I was thinking that right before we got on our call. I was at my campus office today. What used to be so much of my normal day seemed strange. The school keeps bringing people back to the offices, but then someone contracts COVID, and we go back to working from home. They plan on bringing kids back to start the fall semester, but the staff has a pool going on when that ends, and all teaching goes back to virtual. I'm not sure what 'normal' is anymore."

"My walk-through nature helped me remember normal for a bit," said Trey. "I have a spiritual side to my life, and I needed the time and quiet to get in touch with it again. While we have the capability of going a hundred miles an hour with our life, I don't believe we should be going at that pace all the time. There is a line in the Bible that goes, "Be still and know that I'm God." I don't care what people believe, but we all need that quiet to get in touch with ourselves. I hope I remember my own lesson when things get crazy."

"You know the group of people I get jealous of?" asked Felicia. "Europeans. Many countries in Europe give their workers six weeks of vacation and make them take it. As far as I know, it doesn't hurt their productivity."

"It's funny you said that" said Trey. "I studied how Europe works when I did my doctorate. Our culture has brainwashed us into believing that the American work ethic is something we should all aspire to. Well, for many, that work ethic means working our butts off 24/7 with no time off."

"I remember a car commercial that kept appearing when the Olympics were on TV. I don't even remember the car, but the actor doing the commercial had the appearance of a successful businessman and touting that Americans take pride in how we work and that vacations aren't in our vocabulary." Felicia paused for a second. "I hated that commercial. It was everything wrong with how we conduct business."

Trey said, "I'm glad to hear you say that. Let me ask you, Felicia, when was your last vacation?"

"Uh, I took a few days off at Christmas," said Felicia.

"No, I mean a real vacation where you took a week or two and got out of town and enjoyed yourself," insisted Trey.

Felicia thought hard. Then she picked up her phone. Trey asked, "What are you doing?"

"I have to go back through my calendar and see."

"Stop! If you have to do that, then it's been too long. You know what diminishing returns mean, correct?" asked Trey.

"Yes, just because you do something more often, it doesn't mean that the results continue to become greater."

"You have that right. Do you know that studies along those lines led to adopting the 40-hour workweek in this country? Scientists showed that people working much past that many hours resulted in a decline in production, especially when more people worked more hours week after week without a break."

"I would love to work a 40-hour week now," said Felicia.

"I'll say," said Trey. "Remember a month ago when we talked about how racism seems to have gone backward in this country. Well, how we work has seemed to regress too. We have this concept in America that more is always better. I love pizza, but if I ate it every day, I would weigh 300 pounds and be decidedly unhealthy. We are doing the same thing with work. We have both talked about working 80-hour weeks sometimes. Exactly where has that gotten us?"

Felicia had to think about that. "In the grand scheme of things, nowhere."

"Were you ever thanked for all that extra work?"

"Not really," answered Felicia, "but I had to get a task done."

"Granted," said Trey, "and those situations arise. The mistake we make is that it becomes our new normal of working. In the long run, it is only going to wear us out."

"You know, I have not really thought about this before," said Felicia.

"Yes, because you don't take the time to chill and think about life," said Trey. "And I don't mean you in particular but most people. You once talked about being on a hamster wheel. I propose we must mindfully step off that wheel from time to time to fully appreciate where we are, where we have been, and where we want to go."

"Geez, you spend three days in the woods, and you become a sage. The thing is, I know you are absolutely right. I have to think about this in my life. I'm not sure what I can do about it, though," Felicia said.

"I concluded while meandering through the woods last week that it comes down to setting boundaries. We all get vacation time; we need to take it. Furthermore, when we are in a place where we supervise others, we owe it to them to encourage them to take time off. We'll get rested and refreshed people when they return to work."

"I'm writing this all down," said Felicia picking up a pen.

"Here's one more for you, then. As I pondered all of this while hiking, I thought back to one of our recent conversations. You are in a position where you are making a difference in eliminating institutionalized discrimination at your university, correct?"

"Sure," said Felicia, "I'm trying to do away with any racial and gender bias in how we hire and promote."

Trey said, "Then you are in a place to enforce some of this philosophy concerning how people work at your place. You can be an advocate to make sure people take the time to recharge their batteries and not only pay it lip service."

Sitting back, Felicia said, "I guess I can make a difference there too."

"As a wise woman once said to me, we sometimes have to take baby steps to make a difference," concluded Trey.

Courageous Reflections

Now that you have read "The Transition on the Green Pond":

- What resonated with you?

- What caused you to think and ponder?

- What made you curious to investigate further?

- What notes could you jot down?

- Have you ever dealt with people working too hard or spending too much time in your business or under your responsibility?

- How do you respond when confronted with burnout in any form?

- What action(s)/goal(s) could you take to experience the best outcome of dealing with the well-being in your professional life, personal life, and dealing with the Damndemic?

- What's your plan, and when do you start, and how will you know when you have achieved your goals?

Reflection Notes

Chapter 8
Call to Action
#notoriousrbg #johnrlewis

Trey and Alyse sat next to each other on the couch, watching the tribute to the late Supreme Court Justice, Ruth Bader Ginsberg. She had died the day before, and they watched the show detailing her life story and accomplishments. When it was over, Trey clicked the television off.

"She was one hell of a person," said Trey.

"She was one hell of a woman," corrected his wife. "She was on the cutting edge of showing that women could be on an even footing with men in the workplace. I forget how these women before me allowed me to be where I'm in business. They were the trailblazers."

"I can't deny that" said Trey. "I admit, as a man, I'm not really up on who did what for bringing women up to the same level as men."

"Well, before you get full of yourself, I have something earth-shattering to tell you. We aren't there yet!" stated his wife.

She continued looking at Trey incredulously. "Really? On average, women still don't make what a man makes in most jobs and professions. We aren't in as many board rooms or leadership positions as we should be, and there are still plenty of men who think we are around to keep house and have babies. To them, we only have a job as a hobby. Forget that women head up more households and are the primary wage earners for many families."

Trey reached over to the coffee table and picked up a white napkin. He waved it in the air. Alyse looked at him, suspiciously and said, "What are you doing?"

"I'm surrendering. I didn't know you felt so strongly about this."

Alyse looked quietly at Trey for a minute and said, "You're an idiot."

"Then she said that I'm an idiot," said Trey.

"She's right. I hope you don't think I'm going to take your side on this," said Felicia. Their conversation started with Trey telling her about the discussion he and Alyse had after watching the special on Ruth Bader Ginsberg.

"Uh, I guess not," said Trey lamely. "I thought you women were doing okay."

He watched his laptop screen in surprise as Felicia doubled over in laughter. When she slowed her laughter down, Trey said, "You know, I'm starting to get an inferiority complex here."

"As you should," said Felicia. "You're a man." She went into hysterics again when she saw Trey's crestfallen face. Finally, she got control of herself and sputtered, "I'm sorry. That was a cheap shot, but I couldn't resist. Listen, even for you enlightened males, you don't know what women face because, well, because you aren't a woman. Yes, we have made huge strides over the past several decades, but we aren't even close to having equality with men in the workplace."

Trey sat there quietly, and the two stared at each other. Felicia broke the silence. "Trey, are you okay?"

He sighed. "Apparently, I haven't anything to add to this conversation."

Felicia said, "Look at it as being educated on two levels, Trey. The first is on the actual subject of how women look at our world. There's still a long way to go. Now, look at it as a lesson in how we need to communicate with others. You truly are an enlightened man, but your understanding of women's issues goes only so far. That means Alyse or me or another woman can add to your education. Take that and think about one of your white friends. He or she might be extremely empathetic to the issue of racism, but they probably don't know how you or anyone of color deal with it on a daily basis. That's where you have to further his or her education."

Trey let that sink in, slowly nodding. "Wow, you do have a talent of holding a mirror up to people, or at least, me," said Trey. "You are right. I have talked to white people who are very much against racism, but there was a bit of a disconnect between us on the subject. I guess that's the missing puzzle piece."

"Talking with someone who isn't exactly in your shoes is always going to present some obstacles that affect how you discuss certain issues. I wasn't even in the room, and I know how Alyse felt talking to you. See, that is how great a woman Ruth Bader Ginsberg is. Even though RBG is gone, she was the catalyst to conversations reminding you that you don't know everything!" Felicia broke out in another fit of laughter.

Trey waved his hands at the screen. "I get it! I surrender again! I'll pick your brains, so I have more insight into what women are fighting for in their lives."

Felicia stopped and wiped tears from her eyes. "I won't bring it up anymore. Thanks for the entertainment value of today's discussion, though." She composed herself and continued. "Putting aside how much fun it is to give you a hard time, RBG was something, wasn't she?"

"I can't deny that" said Trey. "I never realized how monumental her participation in the Supreme Court was. I have been listening to how the Court will become more conservative, which scares me after I saw her impact. We talk about the Damndemic being a marathon without a finish line, but our country seems like a nonstop rollercoaster. I'm beginning to wonder when we are going to stop going down a dip."

"You and the rest of the country," said Felicia. "It amazes me how much we lost in the space of a couple of months with the death of a black man and a white woman. The United States is worse off with their passing.

Trey said, "I guess you are talking about Congressman John Lewis."

"You got that right," said Felicia. "In their own way, they were lions of the institutions where they worked. John Lewis was one of the few politicians left who could directly trace his civil rights roots to Martin Luther King. I find it troubling that he died in this miserable year of 2020 when the subject of racism is so much at the forefront of people's minds. We need voices like his. We need people like him who took their voices and used them to reach a position where they could do good, like Congress for Mr. Lewis."

"I know neither of them died from COVID, but it is another reason to detest this Damndemic. It seems whatever could go wrong in 2020 did," said Trey.

"Shhh," said Felicia, putting a finger against her lips. "I'm not superstitious, but this year isn't over with yet. I don't even want to think about what else can happen."

"We do have an election ahead of us in November," said Trey.

Now, Felicia put her index fingers into her ears and said, "La la la la la – I don't want to talk about it!"

It was Trey's turn to laugh. "Very mature. Do you do that at staff meetings?"

"I want to at times," responded Felicia. "I really don't want to talk about the election, though. I get into discussions about it with friends and family and want to bang my head against the wall. I have unfriended a couple of people on Facebook because their views are so poisonous that I couldn't bear even to see them in my scroll anymore. I have never seen our country and the upcoming election as divisive as it all is now. I literally get sick to my stomach."

Trey said, "I know when I talk to people older than me, they feel the same way. Most of them seem perplexed that the country they thought they knew is vanishing before their eyes. I'm talking about educated men and women of all races. They become tongue-tied when I ask them to put into words why they think everything has changed."

"I run into the same thing," said Felicia. "I do have to tell you about a conversation I had last year with a professor in the history department. We had a fundraising project in the works to construct a new building for the history wing. I was picking her brain for past students she had that might now be in a position to help. We had a great time talking, and soon we somehow got into a discussion about the 1960s."

"Why those years?" asked Trey.

"It was her specialty. She is African American, and she was part of the civil rights movement. She was 15 when she met MLK and John Lewis in the March on Washington. She came of age in that decade and was launching a class centering on the 60s. She contends that the 1960s ranked up there with the pivotal decades in America's history."

"That's quite a pronouncement," said Trey. He stopped and thought. "Is it true?"

"When you listened to her, you would believe it to be so. She won me over. She said that if you only looked at the Vietnam War, the fight for civil rights, and America expanding its technical knowledge to get to the moon, it would be hard to argue. However, she believed that it was the assassinations of three Americans that made the 60s so important."

Trey racked his brain. "Let us see; there were President Kennedy and Martin Luther King, and…and…darn. I'm coming up blank."

"Robert Kennedy," said Felicia.

Slapping his palm on the desk, Trey said, "Yes!" How could I forget him!" Then he calmed down. "Was Robert Kennedy that important in the scheme of things?"

"I asked Professor Marvin that question. She explained to me that Robert Kennedy had a unique connection with the black community at the time. They loved him. Things were very tense when Martin Luther King died in April of 1968. That year, Robert Kennedy was running for the Democratic nomination for President. He helped bring some calmness to people who were about to explode. When an assassin killed Kennedy two months after King died, it was as if hope died. President John Kennedy brought optimism to almost all races when the decade began. By the time someone killed his brother, the optimism scattered to the wind."

"I remember hearing from relatives about the riots that were occurring all over the country. It sounded horrible. Come to think about it, I guess it sounds a little like what we have been going through this year. Is this why we always hear that history repeats itself."

Chuckling, Felicia said, "Yes, our country is becoming every cliché ever uttered. In one way, though, I gather strength from knowing how bad the 60s were. When Professor Marvin gave me her snapshot of the turmoil of that decade and the fact, we got through it and moved forward as a country, it gives me hope for this Damndemic year."

"While I get the analogy," said Trey, "you think we have the people to replace the RBGs and John Lewis's of the world. We need people like that to make a difference."

"They are out there, Trey. Look in the mirror. The man staring back at you might be one of those towering figures. Now, don't snicker. Most great people don't walk around as kids going, "I'm going to be great when I get older.' It's how people respond to a crisis that can thrust them in the limelight."

"So, you believe that people aren't born great; they become that way?" asked Trey.

"It has to be true for the vast majority of people we consider great. On the other hand, infamous people start as kids too without a care in the world. I'm sure Mrs. Hitler loved her son when he was a little boy. There is nothing in his early history to show he would become the monster that almost destroyed Europe when he got older," Felicia said.

"When you only know people from history books, it's hard to picture them as actual people sometimes. I think that is an advantage of living today. Television showed me who Ruth Bader Ginsberg was so quickly that I can feel her contributions to our lives. The pages of history haven't clouded her," said Trey.

"I understand what you are saying," said Felicia, "and believe me, I was never much of a history buff. Talking with a historian helped me see more than ever the importance of why we should study it. People fifty years from now will look at 2020 and have a better perspective of what we went through. Hopefully, they will be able to talk about how the USA only got stronger from the experience, and we started to overcome some of our issues once and for all."

"Do you think it will happen, Felicia? Aside from the Damndemic, we have racism, more people not meeting their basic needs like food, shelter, and medical, school systems are hurting, and the list goes on and on."

Felicia said, "Did you ever play the game Risk?"

"You mean where you try to conquer the world?" said Trey. "Yeah, I have. In college, we got heavily into the game for a semester. Why?"

"How do you win the game?" she asked.

"You try to have more countries than your opponent. In a lot of ways, it becomes a war of attrition. As long as you have more 'people,' you're probably going to win."

"If nothing else, that's how America will overcome racism and other problems we have," said Felicia. "All you have to do is look at the population numbers in the United States. People of color are becoming larger participants in the voting process. Now, I'm not naïve enough to think that will be enough in itself to make changes. I'm sure there will be different needs and politics involved in bringing diverse groups together, but the statistics show that 20-30 years down the road, those most discriminated against today will be a large voting voice. That's power in a democracy if America hangs onto being a democracy long enough."

Trey shook his head a little. "You play for the long game, don't you?"

"I have always tried to be pragmatic. Besides, it took America almost 250 years to get this far. What are a few more years to try and get it right. For all we know, historians in the future will look at 2020 as the decade that was so pivotal in history that the country turned a corner to make things better for all men and women!"

Courageous Reflections

Now that you have read "Call to Action":

- What resonated with you?

- What caused you to think and ponder?

- What made you curious to investigate further?

- What notes could you jot down?

- Have do you feel about what's going on in our country in terms of gender equality, racism, and other social difficulties we have?

- How do you respond when confronted with social issues in any form?

- What action(s)/goal(s) could you take to experience the best outcome of dealing with social issues in your professional life, personal life, and dealing with the Damndemic?

- What's your plan, and when do you start, and how will you know when you have achieved your goals?

Reflection Notes

_____

_____

_____

_____

_____

_____

_____

_____

_____

_____

_____

_____

_____

_____

_____

_____

_____

_____

Chapter 9
Damndemic Redux
#coronavirus

A utumn was in the air as Felicia looked at the news bulletin on her phone. Coronavirus cases were inching up in her state again. She remembered the doctors on television said back in the summer that there would be another rise of the Damndemic in the fall, and they were right.

As so many people did across the globe, Felicia tried to learn as much about the virus as she could. She marveled at how, in a matter of months, knowledge about the disease went from nothing to the development of vaccines. She hoped whenever they did finalize a vaccine that it would work. Felicia figured a facemask would be a perpetual accessory for women and men for quite a while.

She could not understand those who didn't take the virus seriously. She was grateful the medical profession had better methods than at the beginning of the Damndemic to help someone who developed symptoms when they caught the virus. The percentage of people dying from the disease had dropped, but they were still dying. Catching a highly contagious disease such as COVID was a game of Russian roulette that she wasn't going to play if she didn't have to. She knew from reading firsthand accounts of victims or from talking to colleagues at school who had the misfortune of catching it; you could span the spectrum of no symptoms to being slightly sick to very miserable to ending up in a hospital bed.

Felica shuddered a little. She was good at not experiencing any of that. Her department had reverted to working virtually again. Nobody from non-teaching departments could go on campus as the university figured out how to finish up the semester for the students.

With all these thoughts coursing through her brain, she heard Trey calling over the laptop.

"Hey, Felicia, are you awake? If you want to take a nap, I'll let you go."

Felicia raised her head off the back of her chair and gave a tired smile. "No, Trey, I'm not asleep. I'm not even particularly tired. I feel very weary is all."

"I'm sorry to hear that. How come?" Trey asked.

"I was listening to the news," said Felicia.

"That will get anyone weary. Was it anything special or the state of our country as a whole that made you feel like that?"

Felicia said, "The damn Damndemic is picking up steam again. While they haven't closed things up in my state yet, the government tells us to exercise caution again. The cry is going up about not doing any travel, keep groups small, and keep to your home as much as possible. I have been doing that for months already, but I'm not fond of the thought of being confined for another six months. If I start thinking about Thanksgiving or Christmas, I'll start crying."

"Hey, hang in there, Felicia. I know it is getting worse. My kids have been back to virtual learning for two weeks because too many teachers caught the virus simultaneously. Apparently, many of the teachers went to a happy hour one Friday after school. It didn't turn out to be an incredibly happy time as it turned into a spreader event."

"I'm sorry to hear that. I know you said the kids were so eager to go back to school finally in September," said Felicia.

"They were. Believe me, Alyse and I were ecstatic about it too. Now they are back home. I'm teaching a class of MBA students virtually. One day I picked up what I thought was one of my notes and started reading about the itsy-bitsy spider. The students got a good laugh out of it. I was so flustered, I stopped class soon after that. I laughed later when I told my wife, but that was a moment I felt like I was at the end of my rope. Don't worry, the feeling passes."

"That's a funny story," said Felicia. "I would have enjoyed being a student for that one. Look, I know I'll feel better later. You know how we compare the Damndemic to a marathon where they keep moving the finish line?"

"Yeah, what about it?" asked Trey.

"I recall reading an article where a runner said that all runners reach a point somewhere around the 21 – 23-mile mark in a marathon they call, "The Wall." It's the point where the body is telling a runner to stop, and the runner has to push through it. I'm at my Wall," Felicia said.

"I think we've all hit the Wall several times by now," remarked Trey. "I know you aren't a quitter. Is there something specific that brought this feeling on you?"

"Probably when I had to make the decision that my department is back to working remotely all the time. Everybody was taking a day to come into the office. It wasn't much, but it was a relief to get out of the house for something other than walks or going to the store. As productive as my people have been over the past seven months or so, I felt like I was accomplishing something by getting to our building once a week. Silly, huh?"

"Hey, you are talking to someone who has been in a new job for almost two months and still hasn't set foot in his office. To tell you the truth, I could head over to the University of Chicago right now and not even be able to locate my office. Sometimes it bothers me, but I have two elementary kids to help home school to take my mind off it," Trey said sarcastically.

"Thank you," said Felicia, smiling. "You have a talent for taking my pity party and making your life sound worse."

Trey bowed to the computer screen. "It's a minor talent. And you're welcome. Look, we've been going through this craziness for most of the year. We can keep going. Besides, we have no choice."

"You can be such a wise man at times," said Felicia. "I think my biggest regret is I never did take that vacation we talked about when things calmed down in the summer. I keep thinking about the trip you did then."

"Why don't you try taking a week off anyway," suggested Trey. "Shut off your phone, unplug the computer, and let everyone at school think you went somewhere. Then, take some day trips in the area where you don't have a lot of people around. Or stay home and binge watch some indulgent TV series or a bunch of movies. Read a book – they still make them with covers and pages and everything. The important part is to make like you are lost in the Himalayas or something where your department can't reach you."

Felicia sat there quietly. Trey asked, "Stupid idea?"

"No, it might be one of the better ones I've heard in a while," commented Felicia. "Just thinking about a week away from work and dealing with video conferencing and endless phone calls, texts, and emails sounds like heaven."

"We talked before about this," said Trey. "We all need to recharge our batteries. It is hard to do that when you are plugged into work all the time."

"Trey, I'm going to give this some serious thought. I'm also feeling beat-up thinking about all that has occurred in 2020. Do you think things will ever go back to where they were at the beginning of the year?"

"Boy, do you ask hard questions!" exclaimed Trey. "Let's look at what we have been through so far. Do we want to go back to how everything was before the Damndemic started?"

Felicia narrowed her eyes and gazed at him. "Don't we? Is this some kind of trick question?"

"Not at all. I'm not talking about all the social distancing and isolation we've been practicing. People want to see their family and friends. It would be great to have a staff meeting that isn't on the computer screen. I want to shake the hands of my new colleagues. It would be nice to hit a happy hour without taking a COVID test the next day. I think we agree we want that aspect of life back again."

"Without a doubt," said Felicia. "I miss people. I want to go back to the gym again. I have equipment in my spare room, and I have been strict about working out, but it isn't the same as taking a class or seeing friends around."

"Okay, we agree on that. Now I bring the rest of this up because it was part of a project my new university gave me. I pose to you the question – have we learned anything during the Damndemic about conducting business better?"

Felicia gave that some thought. "I think many companies and organizations have learned how to be flexible in so many ways. Telecommuting certainly works, though I'm not sure if it is good to do 100% of the time."

"True, but how about a few days a week? Let's look at your schedule. For the sake of argument, when you went to the campus for an 8:00 AM meeting, what time did you start your day?"

"I would get up at 5:30 to shower, dress, and do that make-up thing us girls would do. I'd stop for coffee on the way, find a parking place, and still have a 15-minute walk to my office."

"Now, if you have an 8:00 AM Zoom meeting from home, what's your time frame then?"

In spite of herself, Felicia broke out in a grin. "On a good day, I'll wake up at 7:30. A touch of makeup, run a brush through my hair, throw on a nice blouse, and I'm ready. My coffee brewer is on a timer, so I know that will be available."

"Think about how much time that gives you for yourself, Felicia. We talk about all the hours we sometimes work, but how much of that is devoted to preparing for the day and commuting. You and I have it easier compared to some. I have friends who have an hour or more commute to work, and that's one way!"

"I certainly see your point on that," said Felicia. "I feel like I get enough sleep these past months than I ever have. I agree, the Damndemic has opened up different ways of doing business."

"It isn't only in the area of telecommuting. Employees that used to spend thousands of dollars of the company's money and spending time traveling long distances discovered they don't have to do that anymore. It would be great to fly to Paris for a business meeting, but now you have a video-conference. Companies love to find ways to cut down on their overhead."

"Working in academia, I didn't think about that too much," said Felicia. "I guess they are saving money."

"If they didn't, they will. They might be paying rent on office space or buildings they lease, but that will stop when the leases run out because they allow most staff to work from home. We both know people who moved to their dream location because they don't have to be tied to their office anymore. For many workers, the Damndemic opened up a lot more flexibility with their work."

"You make a strong case," said Felicia. "However, there are lots of drawbacks to that. Empty buildings, restaurants closing that catered to the workers, a city or area's tax base becoming reduced. There are new problems that pop up."

Trey said, "I know there are downsides to the Damndemic, many of them. But we started this conversation trying to look for positives. Are there any others you can think of where the economy is concerned?"

"I think the entire paradigm of how business is conducted has shifted. I know my UPS guy by name since I have had so many things delivered to me. Other than the grocery stores and an occasional trip to a Target or Wal-Mart, I do all my shopping online," said Felicia.

"Hmmm, I thought only Alyse bought everything via the internet. You know this paradigm shift has changed something else - the carbon footprint we leave from our actions."

"Because we are driving less," said Felicia. "Heck, we aren't flying, cruise ships are sitting at the docks, and I have no idea about trains."

"Exactly! Oil is abundant to the point of a glut on the world market, and the air is measurably cleaner in many parts of the world. The Damndemic has forced people to do what we have been giving lip service about for decades."

"Well, I'm all for a greener planet," said Felicia, "so I guess even a temporary reprieve from all the gases and chemicals we put into the atmosphere is a good thing."

"I'll give you one more thing I think the Damndemic gave us this year. I genuinely wonder if our country would have focused on all the societal issues that we are facing to the degree we have if we weren't sitting at home. They were all terrible and deserve the blowback and protest they fostered, but people did have more downtime to digest what's going on in our country. For whatever reason, we endured a perfect storm that put a spotlight on so many racial issues and other problems we have."

"That's an interesting insight," said Felicia. "I know the different killings by the police would have attracted just as much outrage, but I can see where more people might have spoken up and gotten involved because they had the time. If that is the case, then I guess something positive came out of the Damndemic. It hardly cancels out all the sickness and death the Damndemic brought us."

"You're right," said Trey. "I wasn't trying to say it did. My whole point is that we have adapted and shown our flexibility – both as individuals and organizations. We have to continue doing it a little longer, that's all." Trey flashed a quick smile. "At least, I hope it is only a little longer. I'm trying to give you a pep talk, but I have my days where I want to curl up in bed and wake up when this nightmare is over."

"Believe it or not, you helped me feel better," said Felicia.

"I did?" asked Trey. "I mean, of course, I did. How did I do that?" he inquired softly.

"You reminded me what we have been doing for the past months and that we have it in us to continue moving forward. Neither of us said that the Damndemic showed us how much grit we can have when the going gets tough. Your video calls have been so helpful and sometimes a lifeline to my sanity."

"Right back at you, girl. Same time, next week?" asked Trey.

"No, we'll connect the following week. I'm taking the week off. Felicia out!"

Courageous Reflections

Now that you have read "Damndemic Redux":

- What resonated with you?

- What caused you to think and ponder?

- What made you curious to investigate further?

- What notes could you jot down?

- Have do you feel the Damndemic has affected you?

- How do you respond when confronted with the difficulties the Damndemic brought to you?

- What action(s)/goal(s) could you take to experience the best outcome of dealing with the issues of the Damndemic in your professional and personal life?

- What's your plan, and when do you start, and how will you know when you have achieved your goals?

Reflection Notes

_____

_____

_____

_____

_____

_____

_____

_____

_____

_____

_____

_____

_____

_____

_____

_____

_____

_____

_____

_____

Chapter 10
Perseverance
#staystrong

This book's purpose was to allow the reader to reflect on what they have gone through while dealing with the Damndemic. COVID – 19 is an event none of us have faced. It has affected every corner of our lives.

Occurring concurrently with the pandemic was one of the most consequential presidential elections ever held in the United States. As of this writing, the Presidential election was right around the corner, and I didn't know the outcome. Depending on what happens, it might be worth another book in the future. Regardless of the election results, its ramifications will be far-reaching for a long time.

As we followed Felicia and Trey's conversations, I tried to recreate actual discussions that have been going on between people for months. Their fears and hopes mirror much of what I have heard from others or felt myself. The backdrop of losing some great Americans and America facing its ongoing issue of systemic racism, gender equality, and other matters is as real as I could make it. There are undoubtedly many more significant concerns than these, but they are certainly in the top 10 of the genuine problems we face. Throw in the issues of police indiscriminately shooting people and civil rights not regressing into the 1950s, and you can see I merely touched on a fraction of our difficulties as a country.

I also thought it was valuable to showcase typical workplace dilemmas, and as well as what you do when you are looking for work during a pandemic.

Since this has never happened before, at least not since the 1918 Spanish Flu Epidemic, there isn't any information on the subject.

More than anything, I wanted to convey to the reader much of what Felicia and Trey kept reminding each other – we can get through this mess. I think the analogy of the Damndemic being a marathon with a moving finish line is appropriate. I have no clue when we will get back to normal or what the normal will look like. I do know that if we keep exercising the skills we have that have brought us through other difficulties, they will serve us getting through this unique bleakness that has covered our country.

Felicia and Trey are typical of how people are. They can be optimistic or down in the dumps. Sometimes they can be both during one Zoom call. Most of all, I want people to realize the lesson of Felicia and Trey. They were there for each other. They could discuss all sides of an issue. When one was down, the other would try to pick him or her up. They knew different information and helped each other learn some of their unique knowledge. When it came to mindfulness, there was no judgment about each other, and they had a trustworthy relationship.

We all need this at this time in our lives. In truth, we need it all the time, but especially now. Having a trusted colleague, friend, or family member is a requirement to successfully navigate the ups and downs of life. We should be doing all we can to build others up instead of tearing them down. During times like this, I recall the Three Musketeers motto: All for one, and one for all. Can you imagine how we could navigate life if everyone had this philosophy as part of their DNA?

I believe many people do, but too many have the motto of "All for Me" to throw enough speedbumps into the process of real progress among humankind. Some might think that it is a rather lofty goal to expect people to work together for a common goal of humanity. The thing is it does happen during a time of crisis. We have seen it during the Damndemic. By mindfully pursuing that attitude all the time, imagine what we can achieve!

Okay, I'm not going to get everyone working together. However, I challenge each of my readers to mindfully take on being the best you can be at all times. The Damndemic has shaken many of our foundations, so I don't expect you all to jump on board with this at once. Find a support partner like

Felicia and Trey were for each other. Read or take courses to improve those areas of your life you want to improve. Do what you can to positively affect others in your life, which also means your work life. We live an organic life, and everything we do is connected. You cannot truthfully separate one part of your life from another.

We are all in this together. I don't have all the answers, but I believe in you and those I have worked with and helped over the years. The Damndemic is an obstacle, but it will eventually move away. Until then, we will do all we can to survive and thrive.

We got this!

Courageous Reflections

Now that you have read the book, let us do one more reflection; one that is more in-depth than the chapter reflections.

- How did the pandemic restrictions affect your interaction with family or friends?

- Is telecommuting or zooming the same as interacting in person with someone? If not, why not?

- What was your life happening moment/event during the Covid-19 pandemic that you would like to share?

- Do you have more available time during the Damndemic? If so, how are you using it?

- It may be a time for self-reflection. If you want to grow personally, professionally, and spiritually, what will you do with your time to grow in these areas?

- What's your plan, and when do you start and how will you know when you have achieved your goals?

Reflection Notes

_____

_____

_____

_____

_____

_____

_____

_____

_____

_____

_____

_____

_____

_____

_____

_____

_____

_____

_____

_____